Entrepreneurship and the Informal Sector

This book contributes to the ongoing discussion around entrepreneurship in Africa and how it can be made more sustainable. The chapters included highlight the need to consider the grey area between private and public sector dichotomy, which has been the focus of previous research efforts. The contributors to this book offer an intersectional view of entrepreneurship and widen the lens of inquiry to include informal sectors in discussions pertaining to innovation in business. The individual chapters consider economic and sociocultural contexts, the role of gender, the effect of militancy on entrepreneurship and informal small and medium enterprises. By doing so, this book argues that the neglect accorded to the informal and self-employment sectors may have hampered African business development in various ways. This book is a significant new contribution to studying informality in relation to business and entrepreneurship. It will be of interest to researchers and advanced students of business, economics, politics, sociology, public policy, and development studies.

This book was originally published as a special issue of the *Journal of African Business*.

Nnamdi O. Madichie is Professor of Marketing and Entrepreneurship and Coordinator of the Center for Economic Governance and Leadership at the University of Kigali, Rwanda. He is also Research Fellow at the Bloomsbury Institute in London and Visiting Professor at both the Unizik Business School and Coal City University, Nigeria.

Ayantunji Gbadamosi is Associate Professor of Marketing and Co-chair for the School Research Ethics Committee at the Royal Docks School of Business and Law at the University of East London, UK.

Pantaleo D. Rwelamila is Professor of Project Management and Project Procurement Systems at the Graduate School of Business Leadership at the University of South Africa (UNISA), Pretoria, South Africa.

Entrepreneurship and the Informal Sector

Challenges and Opportunities for African Business Development

Edited by
Nnamdi O. Madichie, Ayantunji Gbadamosi
and Pantaleo D. Rwelamila

LONDON AND NEW YORK

First published 2023
by Routledge
4 Park Square, Milton Park, Abingdon, Oxon, OX14 4RN

and by Routledge
605 Third Avenue, New York, NY 10158

Routledge is an imprint of the Taylor & Francis Group, an informa business

Chapters 1–4 and 6 © 2023 Taylor & Francis
Chapter 5 © 2021 Paul Agu Igwe and Chinedu Ochinanwata. Originally published as Open Access.

With the exception of Chapter 5, no part of this book may be reprinted or reproduced or utilised in any form or by any electronic, mechanical, or other means, now known or hereafter invented, including photocopying and recording, or in any information storage or retrieval system, without permission in writing from the publishers. For details on the rights for Chapter 5, please see the chapters' Open Access footnotes.

Trademark notice: Product or corporate names may be trademarks or registered trademarks and are used only for identification and explanation without intent to infringe.

British Library Cataloguing-in-Publication Data
A catalogue record for this book is available from the British Library

ISBN13: 978-1-032-39204-2 (hbk)
ISBN13: 978-1-032-39227-1 (pbk)
ISBN13: 978-1-003-34890-0 (ebk)

DOI: 10.4324/9781003348900

Typeset in Minion Pro
by codeMantra

Publisher's Note
The publisher accepts responsibility for any inconsistencies that may have arisen during the conversion of this book from journal articles to book chapters, namely the inclusion of journal terminology.

Disclaimer
Every effort has been made to contact copyright holders for their permission to reprint material in this book. The publishers would be grateful to hear from any copyright holder who is not here acknowledged and will undertake to rectify any errors or omissions in future editions of this book.

Contents

Citation Information vi
Notes on Contributors viii

1 Entrepreneurship and the Informal Sector: Challenges and Opportunities for African Business Development 1
   Nnamdi O. Madichie, Ayantunji Gbadamosi and Pantaleo D. Rwelamila

2 Women Entrepreneurship and Poverty Alleviation: Understanding the Economic and Socio-Cultural Context of the Igbo Women's Basket Weaving Enterprise in Nigeria 8
   Ugochukwu Chinonso Okolie, Christian Ehiobuche, Paul Agu Igwe, Michael Austin Agha-Okoro and Chukwuemeka Christian Onwe

3 Entrepreneurial Competencies and the Performance of Informal SMEs: The Contingent Role of Business Environment 28
   Ayodotun Stephen Ibidunni, Oyedele Martins Ogundana and Arinze Okonkwo

4 Against the Norm? Entrepreneurial Human Capital, Gender and Resource Mobilization in Sub-saharan Africa 51
   Ikenna Uzuegbunam, Rachida Aïssaoui and Amy Taylor-Bianco

5 How to Start an African Informal Entrepreneurial Revolution? 74
   Paul Agu Igwe and Chinedu Ochinanwata

6 The Effect of Militancy on Local and Informal Enterprises in Developing Countries: Evidence from Niger Delta 92
   Ignatius Ekanem, Terence Jackson and Ayebaniminyo Munasuonyo

Index 111

Citation Information

The chapters in this book were originally published in the *Journal of African Business*, volume 22, issue 4 (2021). When citing this material, please use the original page numbering for each article, as follows:

Chapter 1
Entrepreneurship and the Informal Sector: Challenges and Opportunities for African Business Development
Nnamdi O. Madichie, Ayantunji Gbadamosi and Pantaleo D. Rwelamila
Journal of African Business, volume 22, issue 4 (2021) pp. 441–447

Chapter 2
Women Entrepreneurship and Poverty Alleviation: Understanding the Economic and Socio-cultural Context of the Igbo Women's Basket Weaving Enterprise in Nigeria
Ugochukwu Chinonso Okolie, Christian Ehiobuche, Paul Agu Igwe, Michael Austin Agha-Okoro and Chukwuemeka Christian Onwe
Journal of African Business, volume 22, issue 4 (2021) pp. 448–467

Chapter 3
Entrepreneurial Competencies and the Performance of Informal SMEs: The Contingent Role of Business Environment
Ayodotun Stephen Ibidunni, Oyedele Martins Ogundana and Arinze Okonkwo
Journal of African Business, volume 22, issue 4 (2021) pp. 468–490

Chapter 4
Against the Norm? Entrepreneurial Human Capital, Gender and Resource Mobilization in Sub-saharan Africa
Ikenna Uzuegbunam, Rachida Aïssaoui and Amy Taylor-Bianco
Journal of African Business, volume 22, issue 4 (2021) pp. 491–513

Chapter 5
How to Start African Informal entrepreneurial revolution?
Paul Agu Igwe and Chinedu Ochinanwata
Journal of African Business, volume 22, issue 4 (2021) pp. 514–531

Chapter 6
The Effect of Militancy on Local and Informal Enterprises in Developing Countries: Evidence from Niger Delta
Ignatius Ekanem, Terence Jackson and Ayebaniminyo Munasuonyo
Journal of African Business, volume 22, issue 4 (2021) pp. 532–549

For any permission-related enquiries please visit:
http://www.tandfonline.com/page/help/permissions

Notes on Contributors

Michael Austin Agha-Okoro, Social and Environmental Forestry, Federal University of Agriculture, Markudi, Nigeria.

Rachida Aïssaoui, Department of Management, College of Business, Ohio University, Athens, USA.

Christian Ehiobuche, School of Business, Stockton University, USA.

Ignatius Ekanem, Middlesex University Business School, The Burroughs, London, UK.

Ayantunji Gbadamosi, School Research Ethics Committee, Royal Docks School of Business & Law, University of East London, UK.

Ayodotun Stephen Ibidunni, Department of Business Administration, Chrisland University, Abeokuta, Nigeria.

Paul Agu Igwe, Lincoln International Business School, University of Lincoln, UK.

Terence Jackson, Middlesex University Business School, The Burroughs, London, UK.

Nnamdi O. Madichie, Center for Economic Governance and Leadership, University of Kigali, Rwanda.

Ayebaniminyo Munasuonyo, Middlesex University Business School, The Burroughs, London, UK.

Chinedu Ochinanwata, Lincoln International Business School, University of Lincoln, UK.

Oyedele Martins Ogundana, Department of Accounting and Finance, Nottingham Business School, Nottingham Trent University, UK.

Ugochukwu Chinonso Okolie, Department of Vocational and Technical Education, Alex Ekwueme Federal University Ndufu-Alike, Ikwo, Nigeria.

Arinze Okonkwo, Department of Business Management, Covenant University, Nigeria.

Chukwuemeka Christian Onwe, Department of Management, University of Nigeria, Nigeria.

Pantaleo D. Rwelamila, Graduate School of Business Leadership, University of South Africa, Pretoria, South Africa.

Amy Taylor-Bianco, Department of Management, College of Business, Ohio University, Athens, USA.

Ikenna Uzuegbunam, Department of Management, College of Business, Ohio University, Athens, USA.

Entrepreneurship and the Informal Sector: Challenges and Opportunities for African Business Development

Introduction

Intersectionality of entrepreneurship has attracted significant scholarship effort over the years (Davidson, Fielden, & Omar, 2010; Gbadamosi, 2015, 2019, 2020; George, Khayesi, & Haas, 2016; Hack-Polay, Igwe, & Madichie, 2020; Ingenbleek, 2019; Madichie, 2009; Madichie, Nkamnebe, & Ekanem, 2020; McGrath et al., 1992; Rwelamila & Ssegawa, 2014; Sospeter et al. 2014). However, the discourse of entrepreneurship has been saddled by the liability of informality and/or smallness especially when the conversation is had in the context of Africa. Such baggage are predominantly funding or credit contingent. Indeed, research has long shown that funds have been more readily available for businesses in the 'formal economy,' despite the bulk of small or informal business activities catering to a significant proportion of the population in developing countries (up to 60% in some African economies, see for example, Madichie, 2005; Madichie et al., 2020; Madichie & Nkamnebe, 2010; Minnis, 2006; Nkamnebe & Madichie, 2010).

Furthermore, the numerous independent and unregistered businesses in the informal economy across the globe have been reported to contribute as much as 60% of global economic output (Madichie et al., 2020). In the specific case of Nigeria, the International Monetary Fund (see Medina et al. 2017) indicates that the Nigerian informal economy grew at the rate of 8.5% between 2015 and 2017 and accounted for 65% of GDP. This figure had not changed much prior to the onset of the global pandemic in 2020 (Etim & Daramola, 2020). Therefore, the informal sector in Nigeria, like many other African countries, presents a significant sector that has helped to absorb unemployment in the labor market – albeit still a marginalized segment of the economy. Davies & Thurlow (2010) suggest two reasons for this marginalization. Firstly, there is a general notion of two sectors of the economy: the private sector and the public sector, neglecting the informal. Secondly, the education systems train students to be employed thus, neglecting self-employment or entrepreneurship.

It is our collective view that the neglect of the informal sector coupled with the below par attention afforded to the informal and/or self-employment sector, may have hampered African business development. In the light of these, this special issue seeks to contribute to the ongoing discussion as to how entrepreneurship in Africa can be made more sustainable, and perhaps highlight the need to consider the gray area between private and public sector dichotomy that has been the focus of previous research efforts.

Prior studies in African business

It is positive to note that the subject of entrepreneurship has been gaining ground in the business literature and journal outlets. The network of Kuada (2009), Spring (2009),

Rutashobya, Allan, and Nilsson (2009), Madichie (2009), and Otoo et al. (2012) highlights the popularity of the subject matter of entrepreneurship research in the *Journal of African Business*. This intellectual structure of entrepreneurship research shows the use of social networks as a management theory in the contextual settings of Ghana (Kuada, 2009), Nigeria (Madichie, 2009), Tanzania (Rutashobya et al., 2009), and Niger (Otoo et al., 2012).

The knowledge base of the journal also depicts the relevance of the examination of female entrepreneurship in formal and informal sectors (Spring, 2009; Madichie, 2019; Madichie et al., 2017). Similarly, drawing upon data from across 41 African countries covering the period from 2006 to 2013, Williams and Kedir (2017) evaluated the links between starting up unregistered and future firm performance in Africa. The widespread assumption has been that firms starting up unregistered in the informal economy suffer from poor performance compared to those starting up registered and in the formal economy.

In his bibliometric analysis of "Twenty Years of the Journal of African Business," Kabongo (2019, p. 4) points out that although a number of works debate entrepreneurship, entrepreneurs, and small business enterprises, the financial performance of African public and private institutions is the subject of analysis of various most-cited papers. According to him, the most-studied themes could be grouped into 4 clusters – notably: Examination of the performance and infrastructure of the financial and banking institutions; Research on entrepreneurial opportunities and their implications for individual, organizational, and regional economic development; The competitiveness within the African market and the participation of African firms in global trade; and Analysis of organizations and institutions as primary units of economic and human development.

This special issue extends prior studies (Kabongo, 2019; Zoogah, 2008; Spring & Rutashobya, 2009; Sigue 2011, 2019) in the last decade exploring how organizations in the informal sector can contribute to the economic and human development of Africa (see cluster four above), and how their competitiveness can be improved upon both within and outside the sub-region (cluster three above).

It is noteworthy, therefore, that the marginalization of the informal sector in Africa is not an across-the-board issue, as differences have been observed between indigenous and migrant businesses in Africa. For example, unlike their immigrant counterparts, indigenous Africans have tended to be slower in leveraging the potential of the wider economic system. Concerning the immigrants, research has highlighted this trend of informal businesses among two particular groups – the Chinese and the Lebanese (see for example, Madichie, 2010; Madichie & Nkamnebe, 2010; Madichie et al., 2020; Lituchy, 2019).

On the one hand, Chinese immigrant entrepreneurs have been able to respond to opportunities and challenges in the host business environment in Africa (see Ndoro, Louw, & Kanyangale, 2019; Madichie & Hinson, 2015). The Lebanese on the other hand, have demonstrated an enviable level of "tenacity and risk," which has enabled them to shed the burden of foreignness, as shown by their entrepreneurial endeavors in West Africa (Walker, 2010; Madichie, 2005; Madichie, 2010; Ogunyankin, 2018; Igwe, Ochinanwata, & Madichie, 2020).

In the light of these, and building on the core themes on informality from the *Entrepreneurship, Small Business and the Informal Sector in Africa* Track of the

Academy of African Business & Development (AABD) conference, the guest editors solicited manuscripts that address questions such as:

- What are the intersections between entrepreneurship and the informal economy in Africa?
- What are the opportunities and challenges of formalizing the informal economy for entrepreneurial development in Africa?
- What are the leading and/or lagging entrepreneurially oriented sectors within the informal economy in Africa?
- Is informality good or bad for African entrepreneurship?
- Are there gender disparities in entrepreneurial development of Africa's informal economy?
- Does size matter in the entrepreneurship performance of firms?
- What role can entrepreneurial education play in bridging any real or perceived gaps between the formal and informal economy?

Manuscripts in this issue

Contributions to this special issue spanned across ten institutions (excluding those of the guest editors) - notably Alex Ekwueme Federal University Ndufu-Alike Ikwo, Nigeria; Covenant University, Ota, Nigeria; Federal University of Agriculture, Makurdi Nigeria; University of Nigeria Nsukka, Nigeria; Middlesex University, UK; University of Lincoln, UK; Nottingham Trent University, UK; Metropolitan College of New York; and Ohio University, USA.

The first paper by Ugochukwu Chinonso Okolie et al., entitled "Women entrepreneurship and poverty alleviation," sought to further our understanding of the economic and socio-cultural context of ethnicity and gender enterprise in Nigeria. The authors conducted a qualitative study of 48 Igbo women entrepreneurs who run local basket weaving enterprise in 16 rural communities in the southeast of Nigeria. The study highlights the impact of informal entrepreneurial learning, socio-cultural and economic issues, individual values in business start-ups and development in the cities after post-primary education in an attempt to alleviate poverty in line with Sustainable Development Goal (SDG 1). Findings provide a framework of the Igbo women entrepreneurs' poverty alleviation and show evidence of a perspective of entrepreneurship for poverty alleviation that is different from the mainstream entrepreneurship literature on poverty alleviation.

Ayodotun Stephen Ibidunni *et al.*, in their examination of the performance of informal SMEs and the contingent role of the business environment, used a survey research design based on data from 296 entrepreneurs who operate informal SMEs in Nigeria to conclude that entrepreneurial competencies, especially organizing, conceptual, learning, strategic, opportunity, and risk-taking competencies, are essential for achieving higher innovation performance. The study also points out that the entrepreneurship environment is becoming more endogenous as entrepreneurs, through their entrepreneurial competencies, have started to gain control over it.

Another interesting contribution in this issue is whether human capital, gender and resource mobilization was going against the norm in the African context. In that study, Ikenna Uzuegbunam *et al.*, examined how entrepreneurial human capital affects the resource mobilization process in new ventures, specifically the likelihood of using informal ties (i.e. family and friends) in their hiring process. Building on human capital arguments, these authors theorized that the higher the entrepreneur's formal educational attainment, the greater the likelihood that they will go against the norm of hiring through informal ties. Ultimately the study highlights the need for entrepreneurship education with an emphasis on a regional management education drive.

Still on the subject of entrepreneurial education, Paul Agu Igwe and Chinedu Ochinawata examined the nexus of the informal entrepreneurial ecosystem, from the perspective of ecological resilience. These authors analysed the significant differences between the formal sector, the informal sector, frugal innovations and the supportive ecosystem resilience that produces unparalleled enthusiasm. The study set about developing propositions and a model of productive and unproductive entrepreneurial ecosystems that sought to explain the interactions within the African business environment. Overall, the study posits that as entrepreneurial education and skills increases, there was more likelihood of the creation of formal ventures and growth-oriented micro, small and medium enterprises – moving the informal to formal economy.

Ignatius Ekanem *et al.*, in their study on "The Effect of Militancy on Local and Informal Enterprises in Developing Countries: Evidence from Niger Delta," highlight how Militancy is a continuing process in many developing regions where entrepreneurial activities in the informal economy have the potential to transform lives leading to sustainable development through local initiatives. Often militancy originates in protest against global encroachment and defending the livelihoods of local communities. Yet this leads to detrimental effects on such initiatives. The study focuses on small and medium sized enterprises in the Niger Delta in Nigeria and looks at how the lessons learned may be used in other developing regions facing similar issues. Findings suggest how violent conflict resulting in adverse impact on enterprise development can be mediated by collective actions.

Conclusions

It has been a rewarding experience editing this special issue with diverse insights from authors across Africa, Europe and North America and representing a range of universities to explore some of the challenges of African Business and how these may be addressed. It was interesting to review most of the finally accepted article at least twice. The topics all coalesced around the special issue call on "*Entrepreneurship and the Informal Sector: Challenges and Opportunities for African Business Development.*" The contributions covered conversations and/or debates around Gender – notably *Women entrepreneurship and poverty alleviation; Entrepreneurial Human Capital, Gender and Resource Mobilization in Sub-Saharan Africa*; Competencies and Performance – notably, *Entrepreneurial Competencies and the Performance of Informal SMEs*; and the growing levels of Militancy and their impact on Local and Informal Enterprises in Developing Countries. Collectively, the papers not only do justice to some of the conversations had at the conference for which this journal is the official outlet, but also contribute to the ongoing conversations on African Business Development.

Going forward we would like to see manuscripts covering entrepreneurship and strategy in the informal sector in Africa; entrepreneurial marketing at the nexus of the African informal economy; entrepreneurship and the sustainable development goals in Africa; Gender, Enterprise and the Informal sector in Africa; Informal entrepreneurial education and African Business Development; Sectoral analysis of African entrepreneurship; Intersections of employment practices in the informal and formal sector enterprises in Africa; The informal sector and the African project failure syndrome; Entrepreneurship and the African Continental Free trade Area; and Best practice cases on entrepreneurship and the informal sector in Africa.

References

Asongu, S. A., & Odhiambo, N. M. (2019). Challenges of doing business in Africa: A systematic review. *Journal of African Business, 20*(2), 259–268.

Bräutigam, D., & Xiaoyang, T. (2011). African Shenzhen: China's special economic zones in Africa. *The Journal of Modern African Studies, 49*(1), 27–54.

Davidson, M. J., Fielden, S. L., & Omar, A. (2010). Black, Asian and minority ethnic female business owners: Discrimination and social support. *International Journal of Entrepreneurial Behaviour and Research, 16*(1), 58–80.

Davies, R. & Thurlow, J. (2010). Formal-Informal Economic Linkages and Unemployment in South African. *South African Journal of Economics, 78*(4), 437–459.

Etim, E., & Daramola, O. (2020). The informal sector and economic growth of South Africa and Nigeria: A comparative systematic review. *Journal of Open Innovation: Technology, Market, and Complexity, 6*(4), 134.

Gbadamosi, A. (2015). Exploring the growing link of ethnic entrepreneurship, markets, and pentecostalism in London (UK): An empirical study. *Society and Business Review, 10*(2), 150–169.

Gbadamosi, A. (2019). Women entrepreneurship, religiosity, and value-co-creation with ethnic consumers: Revisiting the paradox. *Journal of Strategic Marketing, 27*(4), 303–316.

Gbadamosi, A. (2020). Buyer Behaviour in the 21st century: Implications for SME marketing (Chapter 5). In S. Nwankwo & A. Gbadamosi (Eds.), *Entrepreneurship marketing: Principles and practice of SME* (2nd ed., pp. 72–96). Oxfordshire: Routledge.

George, G., Khayesi, J. N. O., & Haas, M. R. T. (2016). Bringing Africa in: Promising directions for management research. *Academy of Management Journal, 59*(2), 377–393.

Hack-Polay, D., Igwe, P. A., & Madichie, N. O. (2020). The role of institutional and family embeddedness in the failure of Sub-Saharan African migrant family businesses. *The International Journal of Entrepreneurship and Innovation, 21*(4), 237–249. https://doi.org/10.1177%2F1465750320909732

Igwe, P. A., Ochinanwata, C., & Madichie, N. O. (2021). The "Isms" of Regional Integration: What Do Underlying Interstate Preferences Hold for the ECOWAS Union? *Politics & Policy, 49*(2), 280–308. doi:10.1111/polp.12396

Ingenbleek, P. T. (2019). The endogenous African business: Why and how it is different, why it is emerging now and why it matters. *Journal of African Business, 20*(2), 195–205.

Kabongo, J. (2019). Twenty years of the Journal of African business: A bibliometric analysis. *Journal of African Business, 20*(2), 269–282.

Kuada, J. (2009). Gender, social networks, and entrepreneurship in Ghana. *Journal of African Business, 10*(1), 85–103.

Leandro Medina, Andrew W. Jonelis & Mehmet Cangul (2017) (Eds.) The Informal Economy in Sub-Saharan Africa : Size and Determinants, Geneva: Switzerland, International Monetary Fund, July 10, 2017. https://www.imf.org/en/Publications/WP/Issues/2017/07/10/The-Informal-Economy-in-Sub-Saharan-Africa-Size-and-Determinants-45017

Lituchy, T. R. (2019). Journal of African business – Special issue on the diaspora. *Journal of African Business, 20*(1), 1–5.

Madichie, N. (2005). Corruption in Nigeria: How effective is the corruption perception index in highlighting the economic malaise? *World Review of Science, Technology and Sustainable Development, 2*(3–4), 320–335.

Madichie, N. (2009). Breaking the glass ceiling in Nigeria: A review of women's entrepreneurship. *Journal of African Business, 10*(1), 51–66.

Madichie, N., & Hinson, R. E. (2015). Women entrepreneurship in Sub-Saharan Africa – A case approach. In S. Nwankwo & K. I. N. Ibeh (Eds.), *The Routledge companion to business in Africa*. Chapter 11. ISBN-10: 0415635454; ISBN-13: 978-0415635455. Retrieved from http://routledge-ny.com/books/details/9780415635455/

Madichie, N., Nkamnebe, A. D., & Ekanem, I. U. (2020). Marketing in the informal economy: An entrepreneurial perspective and research agenda (Chapter 26). In S. Nwankwo & A. Gbadamosi (Eds.), *Entrepreneurship marketing: Principles and practice of SME marketing* (2nd ed.). London: Routledge. Retrieved from https://www.taylorfrancis.com/books/e/9780429505461/chapters/10.4324/9780429505461-26

Madichie, N. O. (2010). Understanding consumers in entrepreneurship marketing. In S. Nwankwo, & A. Gbadamosi (Eds.), *Entrepreneurship marketing: principles and practice of SME marketing* (pp. 79-95). Routledge. https://doi.org/10.4324/9780203838648

Madichie, N. O., Hinson, R. E., & Ibrahim, M. (2013). A reconceptualization of entrepreneurial orientation in an emerging market insurance company. *Journal of African Business, 14*(3), 202–214.

Madichie, N. O., Mpofu, K., & Kolo, J. (2017). Entrepreneurship development in Africa: Insights from Nigeria's and Zimbabwe's telecoms. In A. Akinyoade, T. Dietz, & C. Uche (Eds.), *Entrepreneurship in Africa* (pp. 172–208). Brill Academic Publishers.

Madichie, N. O., & Nkamnebe, A. D. (2010). Micro-credit for microenterprises? A study of women "petty" traders in Eastern Nigeria. *Gender in Management, 25*(4), 301–319.

Minnis, J. R. (2006). Nonformal education and informal economies in sub-Saharan Africa: Finding the right match. *Adult Education Quarterly, 56*(2), 119–133.

Ndoro, T. T. R., Louw, L., & Kanyangale, M. (2019). Practices in operating a small business in a host community: A social capital perspective of Chinese immigrant entrepreneurship within the South African business context. *International Journal of Entrepreneurship and Small Business, 36*(1–2), 148–163.

Ogunyankin, G. A. (2018). A "scented declaration of progress": Globalisation, afropolitan imagineering and familiar orientations. *Antipode, 50*(5), 1145–1165.

Olomi, D., Charles, G., & Juma, N. (2018). An inclusive approach to regulating the second economy: A tale of four Sub-Saharan African economies. *Journal of Entrepreneurship in Emerging Economies, 10*(3), 447–471.

Otoo, M., Ibro, G., Fulton, J., & Lowenberg-Deboer, J. (2012). Micro-entrepreneurship in Niger: Factors affecting the success of women street food vendors. *Journal of African Business, 13*(1), 16–28.

Punnett, B. J. (2019). The Commonwealth Caribbean's African diaspora: Culture and management. *Journal of African Business, 20*(1), 41–54.

Rutashobya, L. K., Allan, I. S., & Nilsson, K. (2009). Gender, social networks, and entrepreneurial outcomes in Tanzania. *Journal of African Business, 10*(1), 67–83.

Rwelamila, P. D., & Ssegawa, J. K. (2014). The African project failure syndrome: The conundrum of project management knowledge base—The case of SADC. *Journal of African Business, 15*(3), 211–224.

Sigué, S. (2019). In celebration of the 20th anniversary of Journal of African Business. *Journal of African Business, 20*(2), 155–159.

Sigué, S. P. (2011). Strengthening the position of a premier outlet for African business research. *Journal of African Business, 12*(1), 1–7.

Sospeter, N. G., Rwelamila, P. D., Nchimbi, M., & Masoud, M. (2014). Review of theory and practice literature on women entrepreneurship in the Tanzanian construction industry: Establishing the missing link. *Journal of Construction in Developing Countries, 19*(2), 75–85.

Spring, A. (2009). African women in the entrepreneurial landscape: Reconsidering the formal and informal sectors. *Journal of African Business, 10*(1), 11–30.

Spring, A., & Rutashobya, L. K. (2009). Gender-related themes in African entrepreneurship: Introduction to the articles. *Journal of African Business, 10*(1), 1–10.

Walker, A. (2010, January 25) Tenacity and risk - The Lebanese in West Africa. *BBC News.* Retrieved from http://news.bbc.co.uk/2/hi/8479134.stm

Williams, C. C., & Kedir, A. M. (2017). Evaluating the impacts of starting up unregistered on firm performance in Africa. *Journal of Developmental Entrepreneurship, 22*(3), 1750017.

Zoogah, D. B. (2008). African business research: A review of studies published in the journal of African business and a framework for enhancing future studies. *Journal of African Business, 9*(1), 219–255.

Nnamdi O. Madichie

Ayantunji Gbadamosi

Pantaleo Rwelamila

Women Entrepreneurship and Poverty Alleviation: Understanding the Economic and Socio-cultural Context of the Igbo Women's Basket Weaving Enterprise in Nigeria

Ugochukwu Chinonso Okolie, Christian Ehiobuche, Paul Agu Igwe, Michael Austin Agha-Okoro and Chukwuemeka Christian Onwe

ABSTRACT

This study explores the socio-cultural and economic context in which Igbo women's basket weaving enterprise develops and operates in Nigeria and their beliefs about how entrepreneurial action can alleviate poverty. We conducted a qualitative study of 48 Igbo women entrepreneurs who run local basket weaving enterprise in 16 rural communities of 4 out of the 5 Igbo States (southeast region) of Nigeria, to explore the impact of informal entrepreneurial learning, socio-cultural and economic issues, individual values in business start-ups and development in the cities after post-primary education in an attempt to alleviate poverty in line with Sustainable Development Goal (SDG 1). Focusing on three dominant themes (including socio-cultural and economic issues of the Igbo women basket weaving entrepreneurs, etcetera) from the thematic analysis, we analyze the factors that contribute to understanding the socio-cultural context of the Igbo women's basket weaving enterprise in Nigeria. Findings provide a framework of the Igbo women entrepreneurs' poverty alleviation and show evidence of a perspective of entrepreneurship for poverty alleviation that is different from the mainstream entrepreneurship literature on poverty alleviation.

Introduction

In Nigeria, the Igbo people are known for their highly competitive drive for business both in the rural and urban informal economy (Agu & Nwachukwu, 2020; Igwe, Madichie, & Amoncar, 2020a; Obunike, 2016). Also, ethnic business communities have been explored by many researchers, which have provided a clearer understanding of "the niche contexts of ethnic family small businesses and how they use their social context for competitive advantage" (Igwe et al., 2020a, p. 4). The Igbo, one of the three largest ethnic groups in Nigeria is made up of five states and is located in the southern region of Nigeria (Chukwuezi, 2001). The Igbo people have been referred to as naturally enterprising and ingenious (Igwe et al., 2020b) and "their entrepreneurship is related to a strongly developed pattern of ties between rural and urban kin, circulatory migration, and investment flows" (Chukwuezi, 2001, p. 56). The Igbo people are rooted in culture and their businesses are organized with a strong family pattern (Madichie, Nkamnebe, & Ekanem, 2020; Uduku, 2002). Usually, this is done in an informal and unstructured manner where family members are inducted and trained informally to acquire essential entrepreneurial skills such as buying, selling, negotiation, customer relations, networking, funds management, innovations, market trends analysis, etcetera (e.g., Chukwuezi, 2001; Obunike, 2016; Olulu & Udeora, 2018).

While there is extant literature on entrepreneurial activity, drive and business successes of the Igbo people as well as women entrepreneurship in Nigeria, (Akinbami & Aransiola, 2015; Anugwom, 2011; Dakung, Orobia, Munene, & Balunywa, 2017), there appear to be limited studies on the Igbo women's entrepreneurial action and their belief about how such activities enhance their capabilities and pursuit of entrepreneurship for alleviating poverty in Nigerian context. Also, while many previous studies on women entrepreneurship have either criticized the concept as gender-biased and discriminatory or offer ideas into the possible obstacles of women's entrepreneurship in the global south (e.g., Guma, 2015; Imhonopi, Urim, Kasumu, & Onwumah, 2016; Unruh, Adewusi, & Boolaky, 2014), in-depth qualitative studies of women entrepreneurship in Nigerian rural informal economy has been neglected in social science research. This study, therefore, contributes to women entrepreneurship literature by exploring the Igbo women's basket weaving enterprises and their beliefs about how entrepreneurial action in rural informal contexts can alleviate poverty. Specifically, the current study addresses the following research questions:

(a) What are the social, cultural and economic issues that led the Igbo women to engage in the basket weaving enterprise and the conditions that enhance their entrepreneurial opportunity?
(b) What are the entrepreneurial activities, learning and creativity that develop through basket weaving enterprise and how do these play in a gendered culture, high poverty and inequality society?
(c) What are the outcomes of the Igbo women entrepreneurial action and, in particular, their beliefs about how basket weaving enterprise can alleviate poverty?

Literature review

Entrepreneurship and poverty alleviation

Entrepreneurship has been recognized as a major technique of alleviating income poverty (Igwe, Okolie, & Nwokoro, 2019; Kimmitta, Munozb, & Newbery, 2019; Shepherd, Parida, & Wincent, 2020). Therefore, we are interested in exploring the outcomes of entrepreneurial action by the Igbo women living in the rural communities of Nigeria, and in particular, their beliefs about how entrepreneurial action can alleviate poverty. In this study, we adopt Eckhardt and Shane (2003, p. 336) definition of entrepreneurship as "situations in which new goods, services, raw materials, markets and organizing methods can be introduced through the formation of new means, ends, or means-ends relationships". Also, Ortiz-Ospina and Roser (2016) have explained that poor people live below the metric of income less than $US 1.90 per day. Although, poverty may also involve a variety of other challenges beyond income including capability deprivation, marginalization, discrimination, and poor health (Amorós & Cristi, 2011). Shepherd et al. (2020, p. 6) has explained that "entrepreneurship in the context of poverty is often explored through the lens of necessity entrepreneurship". The authors further noted that necessity entrepreneurship takes place when people start new enterprises because they do not have other employment prospects.

Indeed, the women entrepreneurs in Igbo rural communities do not have alternative employment opportunities and this may have pushed them into being necessity entrepreneurs. While studies on necessity entrepreneurship have offered significant insights into a common type of entrepreneurship, particularly in the global south (Binder & Coad, 2013; Block & Wagner, 2010), it is beyond the focus of this study. Also, while entrepreneurship has been recognized as a useful means of poverty alleviation (e.g., Murphy & Coombes, 2009), which motivated our interest in the subject of the present study, it is important to acknowledge that entrepreneurial activity may not always lead to economic growth (e.g., Alvarez & Barney, 2014; Okolie, Nwosu, & Mlanga, 2019; Sutter, Bruton, & Chen, 2019). We explore these issues by drawing upon Sen's (1999) capabilities perspective and the role of necessity factors such as social (employment), economic (financial), and personal (food security) as enablers of the future prosperity expectations amongst the Igbo rural community women in Nigeria.

Igbo rural community women

According to the World Bank (2020), the recently released 2019 poverty and inequality report in Nigeria, shows that 40% of the total population, or almost 83 million people, live below the country's poverty line of 137,430 Naira ($381.75) per year. Also, Dauda (2016) reported that approximately 54.1% of Nigerian population live in multidimensional poverty with an additional 17.8% being vulnerable to multiple deprivations. In rural Igbo communities of Nigeria, there is virtually no paid employment for people, especially women. The women living in rural communities also face gender-based challenges which include poverty and lack of access to basic social amenities (Croce, 2020; Wood & Davidson, 2011). They are often victims of violence in their own communities (Todd, 2012), tremendously vulnerable and at many risks (Wilson, Gámez Vázquez, & Ivanova, 2012). While the community women are largely socially marginalized (International Fund for Agricultural Development [IFAD], 2004), entrepreneurship has been a major force for their empowerment (Minniti, 2010; Shah & Saurabh, 2015).

The Igbo rural community women entrepreneurs engage in many informal businesses as a key method of alleviating income poverty and mobilization of entrepreneurial initiatives in the pursuit of prosperity (e.g., Belwal & Singh, 2008). However, detail explanation of the many informal businesses that the Igbo women living in rural communities engage in is beyond the scope of this study. Our interest is to explore the outcomes of entrepreneurial action by the Igbo women living in the rural communities of Nigeria, and in particular, their beliefs about how entrepreneurial action can help alleviate poverty. The literature shows that to mitigate poverty and gender discrimination, women need to actively participate in the economic mainstream (Guma, 2015).

The current study is relevant given that the Igbo women's basket weaving enterprise has been an age-long entrepreneurial activity that needs to be explored to understand how the women's entrepreneurial action in rural informal contexts can alleviate poverty. It is important to acknowledge that the experiences of the Igbo women who are into the basket weaving enterprise may not be different from their male counterparts in that they "unite ideas in a way that is consistent with their cultural attitudes towards business" (Ratten & Dana, 2017, p. 62). The Igbo rural women entrepreneurs utilize the resources available within their communities in the pursuit of social and economic sustainability (e.g., Foley, 2000). In line with the concept of women entrepreneurship (Jennings & Brush, 2013) and community-based enterprise (Ratten & Dana, 2017), the rural women entrepreneurs create, manage and develop new businesses for the benefit of their community people (e.g., Hindle & Lansdowne, 2005). Also, the rural women entrepreneurs are self-employed owing to their indigenous knowledge (Ratten & Dana, 2017). Overall, the Igbo rural women entrepreneurs who dwell in their ancestral lands make use of the local resources for their entrepreneurial action, have unique languages and traditions, and maintain social-cultural norms (e.g., Peredo, Anderson, Galbraith, Honig, & Dana, 2004).

The Igbo women's basket weaving enterprise

While the entrepreneurial action among the Igbo people has been extant in the literature, those of the Igbo women in the rural informal contexts have been neglected in social science research. This may be linked to the assumption that women lag behind men in business ownership and economic dependence in the Nigerian entrepreneurship contexts (e.g., Guma, 2015; Winn, 2005). The social and cultural background of the Igbo rural community women enhances their entrepreneurial action, skills and drive, and helps to control their businesses, strengthen their communities by preserving traditions and improve their socio-economic conditions (e.g., Ratten & Dana, 2017). However, while the entrepreneurial action of women entrepreneurs has been documented in the literature (e.g., Cahn, 2008; Daff & Pearson, 2009; Guma, 2015), the focus of the current study is on basket weaving enterprise – one of the major Igbo rural community women dominated businesses that have remained understudied.

Basket weaving has been a major woman-dominated small business for several thousands of families in Igbo rural communities of Nigeria. Thousands of families rely completely on the basket weaving business for earning livelihoods. The local basket weaving industry flourishes in the rural communities in that the raw materials (palm fronds) for the local baskets are readily available and adequate. In the traditional Igbo culture, the palm tree is the most essential economic tree with millions of them in all Igbo communities (Agu & Okagu, 2013). While the current study acknowledges that every part of a palm tree is highly useful for producing wood, palm wine, livestock feeds, edible oil, soap, palm kernel etc., our focus in on the palm fronds which is the only material for the local basket weaving industry in the rural Igbo communities.

Community-based enterprise

The Igbo women who live in the rural community generally face several issues related to poverty, illiteracy, lack of access to social amenities as well as unemployment among others. Therefore, finding innovative approaches to solving these challenges using resources available within their communities has become a matter of urgent concern. Also, to alleviate poverty in rural informal contexts, community-based enterprises such as basket weaving can be further studied to explore how it can be a sustainable means of poverty alleviation – the major interest of the current study. However, Ratten and Dana (2017, p. 66) have explained that "community-based enterprises are a basic foundation of Indigenous society as they emphasize human well-being." The Igbo people dwelling in rural communities have a higher value for their community-based enterprises in that they reside in their ancestral lands, and use the existing social structures for their enterprise outcomes.

We adopt Peredo and Chrisman's (2006, p. 310) definition of a community-based enterprise as "a community acting corporately as both entrepreneur and enterprise in pursuit of the common good". On the other hand, it is important to note that ethnic business is one that the owners or members are tied to a common cultural inheritance. This means that community-based enterprise such as local basketry has an innate competitive advantage due to its unique resources and capabilities generated through family networks (e.g., Madichie, 2011). Also, Igwe et al. (2020a, p. 6) have found that in terms of community-based enterprises, "families provide the learning foundation and support (learning at home, learning in the family business and learning through informal apprenticeship system) that encourages and breed new generations of entrepreneurs". Their finding corroborates the notion assertion that unique elements of the social and cultural contexts of ethnic communities influence their entrepreneurial behavior. This indicates that entrepreneurship has become more relevant to local people as it allows integration of their culture with their businesses. For example, the Igbo rural women entrepreneurs combine personal, community and stakeholder-oriented style of business activity that is mostly not found amid the wider business community.

Methodology

Research setting: rural Igbo communities in Nigeria

Our study setting is women entrepreneurs who run local basket weaving enterprises (sourcing palm fronds materials, processing and weaving into a finished product for agricultural purposes) in Igbo rural communities of Nigeria. Our reasons for choosing this setting are as follows; (a) according to the literature on Igbo entrepreneurship, the Igbo people "provide the learning foundation and support (both learning at home, learning in the family business and learning through informal apprenticeship system) that encourages and breed new generations of entrepreneurs, thus driving the Igbos transgenerational business legacies" (Igwe et al., 2020a, p. 6). Second, we decided to focus on the rural communities in four out of five Igbo states in Southeast Nigeria where palm trees (the only material required for basket weaving enterprise) largely grow – namely, Imo, Anambra, Abia, and Enugu states. In these states, palm trees are the most economic trees for the rural dwellers such that every part of the tree (including palm wine, oil, broom, leaf, timber, kennel, etc.) is of great economic value to the people (e.g., Agu & Okagu, 2013; Apeh & Opata, 2019). Third, a larger number of Igbo women living in these rural communities actively engage in basket weaving as an age-long occupation. Finally, the authors are Igbos, speak the central-local language (Ibo) and have a strong local network, which facilitated the data collection. For example, as native speakers, the authors were able to visit the rural communities (from July to November 2019), interacted with the women in basket weaving enterprise and documented their stories (e.g., Shepherd et al., 2020).

The process of data collection was both challenging and multifaceted: First, due to the insecurity challenges in Nigeria, approaching the rural women into basket weaving enterprise to share their stories was challenging since they were also asked to provide information regarding their finances. Second, it was challenging to identify the local basket buyers in the communities' local markets who export the baskets to other parts of Nigeria for Agricultural purposes. However, to facilitate data collection, we collaborated with the leaders of the local trade unions to identify participants, visits and observations. We, therefore, worked with the local actors to facilitate the process of data collection and improve data quality. The presence of the local actors minimized our impact on the women, helped to assure them of safety and confidentiality, and gained us access to interact and interview them regarding basket weaving enterprise. Overall, this process yielded a total of 48 women (3 women each from 16 communities in the four Igbo states) who willingly accepted to participate in this study. Having the support of leaders of the trade unions provided us with access to participants who willingly shared their stories and provided further access to their family members, business associates and customers. We summarize the data collection process in Figure 1 below.

Data was collected through semi-structured, explorative interviews and field notes (e.g., Shepherd et al., 2020). The main data sources were Igbo women basket weaving entrepreneurs living in rural communities ($n = 48$), and there were two major criteria for sample selection. First, we focused on only women who live in the selected communities and run basket weaving enterprise (weaving local baskets in their homes) as the only source of livelihoods at the time of data collection. Second, we focused on capturing a range of individuals who directly or indirectly involved in the basket weaving enterprise. At the individual entrepreneurial level, we considered the age of the women, education background, and years of their basket weaving enterprise experience. The interviews were conducted at the participants' convenient time and place, particularly, at their homes where they weaved the baskets and at the market where the baskets are sold to buyers who export them to the other parts of Nigeria. This enabled triangulation of data collection by interviewing the rural women basketry entrepreneurs ($n = 48$), their family members (children above 18 years old and husbands; $n = 29$), buyers ($n = 16$) and trade union leaders ($n = 8$).

The interviews with the family members, buyers and trade union leaders specifically complemented and validated the interviews conducted with the Igbo women basket weaving entrepreneurs. Our review of previously published scholarly studies on the Igbo entrepreneurship provided more information from two lenses: "cultural and family factors influencing Igbo business experience and the process of transgenerational family businesses transfer" (Igwe et al., 2020a, p. 9). The interviews with the women entrepreneurs and their family members showed the significance of the next generation and

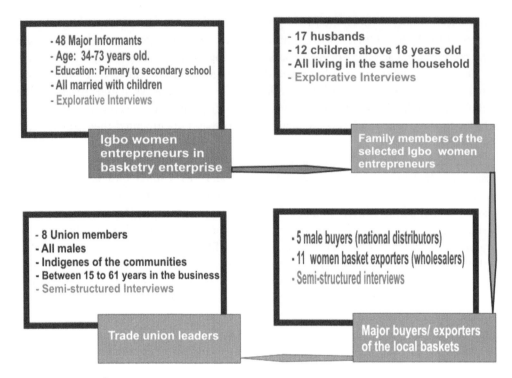

Figure 1. Data Collection Process.

especially, their well-being as they live in poverty. Given the importance attached to their survival in poverty-ridden communities and sustaining their basket weaving enterprise as a means of survival, we collected data on family members. Lastly, because the Igbo rural women entrepreneurs believe in the link between understanding the local market trends and earning money, we collected data on buyers and trade union leaders. All interviews were conducted in the local language (central Ibo) except three buyers who preferred to speak in English language.

Consistent with many qualitative studies (e.g., Okolie et al., 2019; Shepherd et al., 2020) we adopted face-to-face interviews using semi-structured and explorative approaches. We jointly designed our interview guide, reviewed, corrected the interview approaches and translated the interviews prepared in English language into Ibo language. The interview guide focused on the informants' background, living conditions, motives for running basket weaving enterprise, challenges and benefits of running the basketry business in the rural community, and their perceptions of how the basket weaving enterprise can help them to alleviate poverty. During the interviews, participants were allowed to extend the discussion and share more stories. Interviews conducted at the initial stage helped us to adjust the format for subsequent interviews. We recorded all interviews using an electronic device, transcribed the interviews in Ibo language and then translated into English.

The interviews lasted an average of 63 minutes with the women entrepreneurs, 32 minutes with their family members, 52 minutes with buyers and 44 minutes with trade union leaders. The field notes included impressions of the participants, conditions and other contextual information. Also, the interview data were supplemented with observation-based field notes and analysis of previously published scholarly information about Igbo ethnic entrepreneurial action; this enabled the development of rich data for the thematic analysis (Braun & Clarke, 2006). During data coding, which was done using Nvivo-12 Plus, we searched for themes and aggregate dimensions and avoided overlooking important details or imposing our ideas or views on the data. We initially began with open coding which enabled the identification of initial concepts and then grouped the concepts into categories. Also, several steps were taken to ensure that the data remained trustworthy (following Lincoln & Guba, 1985) to ensure data integrity. Second, following Vollstedt and Rezat (2019), we conducted axial coding, which enabled us to focus on the categories and relationships between them and then, helped to develop the themes.

Findings

From the thematic analysis, we presented our findings into three main themes that were identified based on the research questions: (i) socio-cultural and economic issues of the Igbo women basket weaving entrepreneurs, (ii) women entrepreneurial potential and community-based informal enterprises, and (iii) gender discrimination, traditional barriers and playing the role of 'housewife' and 'entrepreneur'.

Theme 1: *Socio-cultural and economic issues of the Igbo women basketry entrepreneurs*

Data from the interviews and field notes indicated a tendency among the women basketry entrepreneurs to improve their living standard by applying creativity in developing businesses based on the available resources at their disposal. They have enhanced their capabilities (skills, knowledge, capital, resources, etc.) by pursuing entrepreneurship for earning a livelihood. These women entrepreneurs also train and nurture their children (next generations) into becoming entrepreneurs through the informal entrepreneurial learning approach. To formally present our findings, we first present the Igbo women entrepreneurship framework that was developed from the thematic analysis (see Figure 2), which highlighted our women entrepreneurship approach.

Our framework shows that these women are highly entrepreneurial and motivated to achieve business successes and alleviate poverty through the elements of informal entrepreneurship in their communities despite facing the challenges of gender discrimination, income insecurity, food insecurity, no formal education and traditional barriers. These women basket weaving entrepreneurs also combine the role of 'housewife' with the role of 'entrepreneur' – a situation that makes them to even work harder to alleviate poverty not for themselves alone, but for their family and the future generations by engaging their children into the basketry enterprise through the informal entrepreneurial learning. The Igbo women entrepreneurs feel successful in their basket weaving enterprise as long as they earn money from sales to pay their community levies, church levies, their children's education fees and other family responsibilities. Majority of the women in the current study explained that before starting their basket weaving enterprises, their circumstances were difficult. This is clearer from one of the informants' narrative:

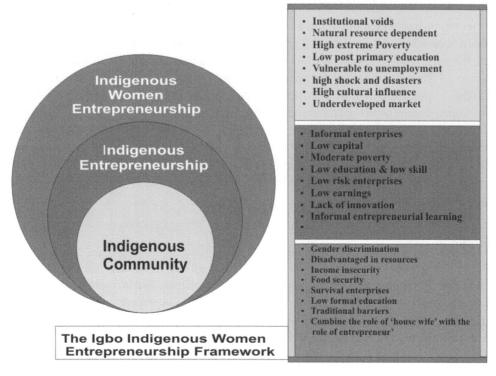

Figure 2. The Igbo Indigenous Women Entrepreneurs Framework.

My husband and I, with our seven children, had never lived in the city. We'd been doing this basket weaving business together as a family business. Our children learned how to weave the basket by watching us. We pay all our bills from the sales of these local baskets (Woman entrepreneur-3).

Our findings suggest that majority of the women didn't attend any form of formal basket weaving training. They acquired the basket weaving skills through informal entrepreneurial learning (simply watch their mothers do it and learn over time). They also appeared to be contented with the little amount of money that the local basket business brings weekly as they rely completely on the basket weaving enterprise for meeting all their financial obligations. Also, starting the basket weaving enterprises is most difficult due to their inabilities to access government loans for small enterprise development. However, our findings suggest that the basket weaving enterprises largely require low capital that can be raised by close friends, relations and nuclear family members. For example, when asked about how they raised capital for their basket weaving enterprise, one of the women explained:

Many of us in this community have never received any financial support for small business development from any government. We raise capitals from friends and families only (woman entrepreneur –23).

When asked how much capital is required to start the basket weaving enterprise, one of the women responded:

> *I started this business with 2,000 Naira. Every other material I needed such as cutlass and knife are already my home properties. I needed the money to pay Palm tree climbers to cut down full-grown fronds for me. With 2,000, I got up to 100 palm fronts* (Woman entrepreneur –12).

For clarity, 2,000 Nigerian Naira is approximately 6. USD To buttress the idea in our women entrepreneurship framework, the Igbo women basket weaving entrepreneurs living in poverty run survival and low-risk enterprises. It was more about how to address their immediate needs (e.g., to earn a little amount of money to solve their immediate challenges such as funding education for the children, supporting the daily life of the family, etcetera). Our findings suggest that the rural women basketry entrepreneurs rely more on the available resources (e.g., palm trees, knives and cutlass) for their basket weaving enterprises. For example, every family own tens to hundreds of palm trees (the only major raw material required to run the basket weaving enterprise). Those who do not have many palm trees may have to purchase from families that own a large number of palm trees within or outside their communities at a steady low price.

However, it became clearer to us that the rural community women's ability to make money depends on their capabilities. In our field note from the visit and interviews with the local basket buyers and trade union leaders, we documented that *"making money from basketry enterprise depends on the women entrepreneurs' abilities; how committed they are to the basket weaving enterprise and the number of baskets they can produce weekly or monthly"*. This agrees with Sen's (1999) capability perspective, which explained that with the availability of resources (e.g., Palm tree), individuals who can function (e.g., entrepreneurial skills in informal contexts) can achieve well-being (e.g., addressing financial insecurity and improving the lives of community people). Also, from our field notes, we found that *"buyers come to the local markets to buy the baskets every four or five days (market days based on the community) for export to other parts of Nigeria, particularly the Northern region where they are highly in use for agricultural purposes"*. During the interviews, one of the buyers explained:

> *[…] so, even if you produce one million local baskets, we are ready to buy all of them here due to the market viability, particularly in the Northern region of Nigeria* (Buyer- 3)

We asked the women entrepreneurs about their efforts toward producing a larger quantity of the baskets due to the market viability, one of them explained:

> *I can produce up to 20 baskets a week and the money may be enough to solve my immediate challenges like buying food items to feed my family. But when I need money to pay education fees of my children, health, church and community levies, etcetera, I simply join forces with all my family members to produce up to 60 baskets a week* (Woman entrepreneur – 42).

Another woman further explained:

> *Local basket weaving is very stressful … so, I can't make a big amount of money if I do the weaving alone. You know that there are many steps in weaving a basket. This is why my children join me in this business. Once they return from school, they'll join me. Through such joint efforts, we produce a larger quantity for sale* (Woman entrepreneur –17).

Our field notes on this participant indicated that *"she can give her children a good basic education, pay their health, church, and security bills and provide food for the family through basket weaving enterprises."* The women wished that their adult children can get quality post-secondary education and get well-paid jobs in the city so that their family can be out of poverty. However, these Igbo women entrepreneurs in the rural informal context defined poverty alleviation in terms of solving their immediate challenges such as providing foods for daily consumption, providing an education for their children from nursery to post-primary education such that the children can migrate to the cities, and run their businesses in the city to financially support their families. Our filed notes suggested that *"there is little emphasis on providing an education for their children to higher education, as this sort of education does not bring immediate financial gains"*. The women entrepreneurs prefer to send their children who had completed post-primary education to the cities to either learn a trade or do 'Nwa Boy' (the Igbo unique form of apprenticeship), with the notion that when they start a trade, they will earn money to support their families. For example, one of the family members explained:

> *My son who has just written the West African Examination Council's senior secondary school examination, schooled from the money we made through this basket weaving enterprise. In the next few months, he'll migrate to the city to start a trade, so that he can help us financially. Attaining higher education is good, but my son will make more money doing business. As for my daughters, they're into the basket-weaving business such that when they marry; they can support their husbands financially* (Family member – Husband).

The quest for addressing financial insecurity and improving lives appeared to have three major dimensions to the Igbo women basket weaving entrepreneurs' drive approach to entrepreneurial action: First: the Igbo women entrepreneurs typically have a high cultural influence. For example, one of the women noted: *"In this community, we have been well known for basket weaving business and other trade. I want my sons to go into trade immediately they complete their secondary education ... so that they can make money faster to support us financially.* In our field notes from visits to this particular woman, we noted that *"all her brothers went into trade immediately they completed their secondary education due to the quest to make money to alleviate poverty."*

Second, due to gender discrimination and traditional barriers, these Igbo rural community women have little choice but to become entrepreneurs. For example, one of the women basket weaving entrepreneurs explained: *"We have some barriers here due to our tradition, male dominance and discrimination against us ... there are so many jobs we can't do in this community as women.* Also, our field notes indicate that the basket weaving enterprise is a *"women dominated business, in that women largely weave the basket, although, their husbands or male adult children can help to take a large number of the baskets to the markets for sale"*. Indeed, the women expressed their desire to contribute to alleviating poverty by becoming entrepreneurs despite the challenges they face in their communities.

Lastly, despite combining their role as 'housewife' with the role of 'entrepreneur', these Igbo women entrepreneurs depend on natural resources in the pursuit of prosperity. For example, one of the women basketry entrepreneurs informed us that *"even though I am a housewife, I work hard to support my husband financially to raise these kids ... I decided to join other women who are into this basket weaving business to contribute to meeting our financial needs."* Based on the above, we present the following baseline proposition:

Proposition one

The Igbo women basket weaving entrepreneurs rely on the available natural resources (Palm tree) in their Indigenous communities for their basket weaving enterprise to alleviate poverty by (a) meeting their basic needs (food, shelter, education of their children, health, church and security levies); (b) They believed that training their children informally into the basket weaving enterprise can enable them to produce more baskets in order to make more money to solve their basic financial challenges; (c) they believed that sending their male adult children to the cities to learn and start a trade immediately after post-primary education is a critical step toward moving out of poverty.

Theme 2: *Igbo women entrepreneurial potential and community-based informal enterprises*

Community-based enterprises are a basic foundation of Indigenous society as they emphasize human well-being (Ratten & Dana, 2017, p. 66). To help their families living in poverty, the Igbo women basketry entrepreneurs in the current study relied heavily on developing efficacy through their communities. In order words, despite the challenges of living in the rural communities, such as poor access to basic amenities, low earning, underdeveloped market, gender discrimination, traditional barriers, and food and financial insecurity, running their basket weaving enterprise in the rural communities appeared to help their basket weaving enterprises. From our field notes, we found that "*a major factor that enabled the women basket weaving entrepreneurship is the strength of their communities. The community-based enterprise such as basketry seemed to flourish due to the nature of the Igbo communities' living conditions.*" To further explore their entrepreneurial potential, we consulted scholarly published articles in reputable journals that are indexed in Web of Science Clarivate Analytics database (see Table 1) for further clarifications.

We found that a major mechanism that enabled us to understand how the rural Igbo women entrepreneurial potential and their community-based informal basket weaving enterprise contribute to the strengthening of their communities includes their exposure to extreme poverty and low earning promotes interaction for strengthening their low risk and survival enterprises. Based on the above findings, we offer the following proposition:

Proposition two

The Igbo women entrepreneurs are embedded in communities, which are shaped by (a) institutional voids and underdeveloped market that promotes creativity among community members, (b) food and income insecurity forces interaction, ideas, informal entrepreneurial learning among the community members, (c) disadvantaged in resources, which forces the community members to rely on the available resources for their survival enterprises.

Theme 3: *Gender discrimination, traditional barriers and playing the role of 'housewife' and 'entrepreneur'.*

Table 1. Igbo Entrepreneurial Potential and Their Community-based Informal Enterprises.

Illustrative quotes	Assumptions
"In the Igbo communities, families provide an entrepreneurial leadership platform, which influences youths through role models, providing mastery experiences and socialization and extended family provides a safe environment for risk-taking, creativity and innovation. Igbos take into business as a means of creating jobs for their children and future generations and as a weapon to develop economic power. Igbos see business as a "way of life" and Informal trade and businesses are common among the Igbos" (Igwe, Newbery, Nihar, White, & Madichie, 2020b, p. 42). "Local trading, local crafts, and wage labour are important in the Igbo economy" (Igwe et al., 2020b, p. 6). "It is notable that Igbo women engage in community-based enterprises and are influential in local politics" (Igwe et al., 2020a, p. 6). "The Igbo trade is mostly informal and unstructured. Igbo indigenous people view entrepreneurship as self-employment of any sort, which bothers on continuously identifying, evaluating and taking advantage of business opportunities and initiating sustainable action to ensure success" (Igwe et al., 2020a, p. 6). "Igbo families are responsible for inculcating on their children the entrepreneurship spirit, creativity and risk-taking" (Agu & Okagu, 2013, p. 4). "Igbo culture recognizes the importance of business and encourages individualist characteristics and the families are responsible for inculcating in their children the entrepreneurship spirit, creativity and risk-taking" (Igwe et al., 2020b, p. 6). "Igbos" have been described as "naturally enterprising people" (Meagher, 2010, p. 25). Thus, in Igbo trade apprenticeship system, even some wealthy families send their children to traditional business schools (Igba-odibo) practice (mostly to trusted relatives, friends or business associates) before providing capital to enable them to start their own businesses (Agu & Okagu, 2013, p. 5). "In the history of Nigeria, perhaps no Nigerian ethnic group is as adventuresome or as enterprising as the Igbos" (Nnadozie, 2002, p. 1). "The Igbos are often cited as the most entrepreneurial ethnic group in Nigeria, their entrepreneurship is related to a strongly developed pattern of ties between rural and urban kin, circulatory migration, and investment flows" (Chukwuezi, 2001, p. 1). "The Igbo tradition encourages individual achievement more than any other Nigerian tribe" (Uduku, 2002, p. 310).	(a) The Igbos address poverty by facilitating informal entrepreneurial learning. (b) Igbos alleviates poverty through trade-off. (c) For Igbos to succeed in businesses, the family is an important factor. (d) The Igbos value their traditional business schools (Igba-odibo) practice. (e) The Igbo rural people rely on the resources in their communities for survival.

Our findings offer new insights into how some challenges such as gender discrimination, traditional barriers and playing the role of a housewife can influence the entrepreneurial drive of the women in the current study as well as their basket weaving business successes. From our field notes on interactions with the trade union leaders, they noted that *"basket weaving business is mainly a business for our community women. You can hardly see men who weave local baskets as a source of income."* This is further explained by a family member:

> *Local basket weaving is one thing that our men do not do ... it is for women. It is laughable seeing our men weave local basket as a source of income. It is not part of our culture. Some things are meant for women and basket weaving is one of them. Although, I can assist my wife in taking the already made baskets to the market for sale* (Family member – Husband –2).

We found that the men's discrimination against women in the basket weaving enterprise either due to tradition or culture makes the women even more successful in the basket weaving enterprise. For example, our field notes indicated that the women "*appeared to be limited to a few small businesses they can do in their communities. Since basket weaving is among the most viable ones, the majority of them went into the enterprise.*" One of the informants explained:

> *I was pushed into the basket weaving enterprise because; it appears to be among the best businesses that my tradition permits women to do in this community. You know ... there are certain businesses I cannot do as a married woman simply because, such businesses are men dominated* (Woman entrepreneur- 8).

Our field notes indicated that "*these rural Igbo community women see basket weaving enterprise as a survival strategy due to traditional barrier and gender discrimination.*" However, the traditional barrier and gender discrimination helped the women to control the basket-weaving business and also to lower the cost of starting and running the enterprise. For example, one of the trade union leaders explained:

> *It is easy to start basket weaving business in the community with a very low capital because the women control the market. Other men dominated businesses are not too affordable to go into. I cannot explain the reasons but this is true. So, there are lots of financial differences between businesses that are mostly run by women and men in this community* (Buyer – 3).

We further explored how the Igbo women basket weaving entrepreneurs combine their roles as housewives and entrepreneurs and found that a major reason for combining their roles has been to help meet their family commitments. While there is the gender division of labor in the Igbo communities, which makes men work to earn money while the women stay at home to make babies, majority of the women in the current study were pushed into basket weaving enterprise because of necessity as they need to support their family and to alleviate poverty. For example, one of the family members emphasized the importance of women assisting their husbands financially in the pursuit of survival and alleviating poverty:

> *Through this basketry enterprise, my mother funded my secondary school education. Although my father is a palm wine taper, the money he makes from wine tapping is not enough. Now, my mother has saved some money through the basket weaving for me to migrate to the city to start and grow my own small business* (Family member- Adult Child - 2).

One of the women further explained:

> *Our tradition encourages women to support their husbands. Therefore, combining my role as a housewife and entrepreneur is an obligation* (Woman entrepreneur – 33).

Based on these findings, we offer the following proposition:

Proposition three

The Igbo rural women go into basket weaving enterprise because; (a) it is supported by tradition, (b) it is a women-controlled business that can be started with low capital (c) they see their roles of being housewives and entrepreneur as obligatory.

Discussion

This study provides a framework of the rural Igbo women entrepreneurs' poverty alleviation that informed how the women who run basket weaving enterprise believed that by engaging in entrepreneurial action, they can help their families out of poverty. The findings of the current study and the resultant framework contribute to women and ethnic entrepreneurship literature. First, our findings offer evidence of a perspective of entrepreneurship for poverty alleviation that is different from the mainstream entrepreneurship literature on poverty alleviation. We found that the rural Igbo women in the current study take a long-term perspective on poverty alleviation (agrees with Shepherd et al., 2020). They do not consider the immediate financial fulfillment from their informal entrepreneurial action, rather they forgo their instant gains for investing in their children's future businesses in the cities upon completion of secondary education under the strong belief that their families (generations) would be out of poverty.

Since the Igbo entrepreneurship system provides entrepreneurial learning that equips the younger generations to take business as a way of life (e.g., Oregiu & Nafiu, 2014), it aligns with the belief of the rural Igbo women entrepreneurs in the current study that by their entrepreneurial action (basket weaving enterprise), their children could alleviate their family's poverty later. Possibly, once the women's children start-up their businesses in the city applying the entrepreneurial skills they acquired through the informal entrepreneurial learning in their families, they can help their families to solve challenges such as food and income insecurity among others. This supports Ratten and Dana (2017) claim that economic self-determination will help Indigenous people to progress economically and socially.

Second, we found evidence that the rural Igbo women's entrepreneurial potentials are rooted in the strength of their communities. Also, we found that the rural Igbo women in the current study benefit from living in their rural communities despite the extreme poverty in that the resources they require to run their basketry enterprise are readily available and natural. Anderson, Honig, and Peredo (2006, p. 3) has explained that "value creation and innovation through local business development are essential means for the alleviation of poverty in communities, and that community-based enterprises are important means for community people to pursue economic development that can both alleviate poverty and sustain the natural environment". For the rural Igbo communities, a community-based enterprise such as basket weaving is relevant to the women. As Ratten and Dana (2017, p. 66) have explained, "community-based enterprises enable the use of existing social structures for a business outcome". We found that these Igbo women value their traditional or cultural heritage and therefore, ensure the protection of their communities to enable the cost-effective business environment.

Third, studies on necessity entrepreneurship have focused on factors that push people into entrepreneurship (e.g., Block, Kohn, Miller, & Ullrich, 2015), and our study supports these previous studies by finding that the rural Igbo women in the current study went into the basket weaving enterprise (one of the community-based enterprises) with the belief that their future generations would be alleviated from poverty. In order words, these Igbo women's struggle for alleviating poverty is not only for their own benefits but their children and their generations. Also, we found that these rural Igbo women entrepreneurs combine their role as housewives and entrepreneurs to support their husbands in the struggle to alleviate poverty; with the intension that their entrepreneurial action would motivate their children's entry into businesses in the cities upon completion of post-primary education to help their families out of poverty. For instance, the rural Igbo women in the current study boost their children's desires for entry into businesses by engaging them in the basket weaving enterprise. This finding supports Matthews and Moser (1996) claim that parents' entrepreneurial experience increases their children's intention to become self-employed. Therefore, our findings suggest that the rural Igbo women in the current study enter the basket weaving enterprise to nurture their children for the future opportunity of alleviating poverty in their generations. Finally, our findings will be of significant benefits to researchers, students, practitioners and policymakers who are in the fields of women, ethnic and Indigenous entrepreneurship to have a clearer understanding of the various paths to poverty alleviation.

Conclusion

The major finding of the current study is that the rural Igbo community women who run basket weaving enterprise are motivated to achieve business success and equip their children with informal entrepreneurial skills to enable their children to move their generations out of poverty. Our study offers many insights into the Igbo women entrepreneurship contexts. For example, our study sheds light on the strength of the rural Igbo communities in facilitating community-based enterprise success. Extreme poverty, gender discrimination, low earning and traditional barriers can promote interaction among the rural community people for entry into survival enterprises. Also, living in rural communities facilitates the basket weaving enterprises success in that it requires low capitals for start-up and the resources required are readily available in the communities. Finally, our framework for the Igbo women entrepreneurship presents reality, particularly, for African researchers working in the field of African and ethnic entrepreneurship. The framework can also be useful for building a theory on women entrepreneurship in the rural community context.

Practical and policy implications

Our findings provide real examples of how entrepreneurship is embedded in unique cultural phenomena. For researchers in the field of African entrepreneurship, ethnic and Indigenous entrepreneurship, community-based enterprises, women entrepreneurship and informal entrepreneurial learning, we hope that the current study would be of immense benefits to their research ambitions. According to Igwe et al. (2020b, p. 10), "the context of ethnic entrepreneurship presents research, policy and practical implications especially given the dearth of research on indigenous and tribal business and policymakers looking for ways to encourage entrepreneurship in African countries as a means of reducing unemployment and poverty." Nevertheless, caution should be exercised when interpreting the findings of the current study in that we are constrained by the generalizability of the findings for other ethnic people living in Nigeria. For those researching on improving the lives of rural community women entrepreneurs, future research on how they can further improve their local community enterprises is important. Another implication is for governments to recognize that rural women entrepreneurs have strong communities that may facilitate governments' policies and action to alleviate the suffering of the people.

Limitations and future research

A major limitation of this study is its focus on the rural Igbo women entrepreneurs who run basket weaving enterprise in their communities. They have demonstrated their skills in using their community environment to their advantage, and the current study studied them. However, we acknowledge a potential limitation of the current study by excluding the rural Igbo women entrepreneurs who do not run basket weaving enterprise and those who are not entrepreneurs yet living in the selected rural communities. Future studies can investigate the differences between the entrepreneurial action of these rural Igbo women entrepreneurs in the current study and those other community-based enterprises. Second, while our propositions may help extend women entrepreneurship theory, they may be subjected to further empirical testing. We encourage future studies to include a larger sample of the rural Igbo women entrepreneurs who run other community-based businesses to test our propositions using an appropriate statistical tool to determine, for example, the extent to which the rural Igbo women entrepreneurs are embedded in their communities. Future research can test the impact of the strength of the rural Igbo communities on community-based enterprises. Also, a longitudinal research design may be adopted to investigate a larger sample of rural Igbo women entrepreneurs' basket weaving enterprise performance and their children's business successes in the cities, and how their entrepreneurial action help to improve the living conditions of their families over time. Finally, our research followed a robust qualitative research approach to contribute to the literature on women entrepreneurship in the African context, and we encourage future researchers to replicate the study using related research methods in their contexts with rural community people.

Disclosure statement

No potential conflict of interest was reported by the authors.

Funding

This work was supported by the African Development Institute of Research Methodology (ADIRM), Nelson Mandela multi-purpose building, Plot 79 Arai River, Independence Layout, Enugu, Nigeria.

ORCID

Ugochukwu Chinonso Okolie http://orcid.org/0000-0002-3069-1784
Paul Agu Igwe http://orcid.org/0000-0003-3624-1861

References

Agu, A. G., & Nwachukwu, A. N. (2020). Exploring the relevance of Igbo traditional business school in the development of entrepreneurial potential and intention in Nigeria. *Small Enterprise Research*, 27(2), 223–239.

Agu, S. C., & Okagu, G. O. (2013). An ethno-archaeologiccal perspectiveon oil palm tree (Elaeis guineensis Jacq) in old Nsukka division of Enugu state. *IKENGA International Journal of African Studies*, 15, 1–19.

Akinbami, C. A. O., & Aransiola, J. O. (2015). Qualitative exploration of cultural practices inhibiting rural women entrepreneurship development in selected communities in Nigeria. *Journal of Small Business & Entrepreneurship*, 28(2), 151–167.

Alvarez, S. A., & Barney, J. B. (2014). Entrepreneurial opportunities and poverty alleviation. *Entrepreneurship Theory and Practice*, 38(1), 159–184.

Amorós, J. E., & Cristi, O. (2011). Poverty and entrepreneurship in developing countries. In M. Minniti (Ed.), *The dynamics of entrepreneurship: Evidence from global entrepreneurship monitor data* (pp. 209–230). Oxford: Oxford University Press.

Anderson, R. B., Honig, B., & Peredo, A. M. (2006). Communities in the global economy: Where social and indigenous entrepreneurship meet. In C. Steyaert & D. Hjorth (Eds.), *Entrepreneurship as social change* (pp. 56–78). Cheltenham, UK: Edward Elgar.

Anugwom, E. E. (2011). Wetin we for do? Women entrepreneurs and the Niger Delta conflict. *Journal of Small Business & Entrepreneurship*, 24(2), 243–252.

Apeh, A. A., & Opata, C. C. (2019). The oil palm wine economy of rural farmers in Nigeria: Evidence from Enugu Ezike, south-eastern Nigeria. *Rural History*, 30(2), 111–128.

Belwal, R., & Singh, G. (2008). Entrepreneurship and SMSs in Ethiopia. *Gender in Management: An International Journal*, 23(2), 120–136.

Binder, M., & Coad, A. (2013). Life satisfaction and self-employment: A matching approach. *Small Business Economics*, 40(4), 1009–1033.

Block, J. H., Kohn, K., Miller, D., & Ullrich, K. (2015). Necessity entrepreneurship and competitive strategy. *Small Business Economics*, 44(1), 37–54.

Block, J. H., & Wagner, M. (2010). Necessity and opportunity entrepreneurs in Germany: Characteristics and earning S differentials. *Schmalenbach Business Review*, 62(2), 154–174.

Braun, V., & Clarke, V. (2006). Using thematic analysis in psychology. *Qualitative Research in Psychology*, 3(2), 77–101.

Cahn, M. (2008). Indigenous entrepreneurship, culture and microenterprise in the Pacific Islands: Case studies from Samoa. *Entrepreneurship and Regional Development*, 20(1), 1–18.

Chukwuezi, B. (2001). Through thick and thin: Igbo rural-urban circularity, identity and investment. *Journal of Contemporary African Studies*, 19(1), 55–66.

Croce, F. (2020). Indigenous women entrepreneurship: Analysis of a promising research theme at the intersection of indigenous entrepreneurship and women entrepreneurship. *Ethnic and Racial Studies*, 43(6), 1013–1031.

Daff, S., & Pearson, C. A. L. (2009). Indigenous employment: The Rio Tinto Alcan initiative in northern Australia. *Contemporary Issues in Business and Government*, 15(1), 1–20.

Dakung, R. J., Orobia, L., Munene, J. C., & Balunywa, W. (2017). The role of entrepreneurship education in shaping entrepreneurial action of disabled students in Nigeria. *Journal of Small Business & Entrepreneurship*, 29(4), 293–311.

Dauda, R. S. (2016). Poverty and economic growth in Nigeria: Issues and policies. *Journal of Poverty*, 21(1), 61–79.

Eckhardt, J. T., & Shane, S. A. (2003). Opportunities and entrepreneurship. *Journal of Management*, 29(3), 333–349.

Foley, D. (2000). *Successful indigenous Australian entrepreneurs: A case study analysis, Aboriginal and Torres Strait Islander* (Studies Unit Research Report, Series 4). Brisbane, Australia: University of Queensland.

Guma, P. K. (2015). Business in the urban informal economy: Barriers to women's entrepreneurship in Uganda. *Journal of African Business*, 16(3), 305–321.

Hindle, K., & Lansdowne, M. (2005). Brave spirits on new paths: Toward a globally relevant paradigm of indigenous entrepreneurship research. *Journal of Small Business & Entrepreneurship*, 18(2), 131–141.

Igwe, P. A., Madichie, N. O., & Amoncar, N. (2020a). Transgenerational business legacies and intergenerational succession among the Igbos (Nigeria). *Small Enterprise Research*, 27(2), 165–179.

Igwe, P. A., Newbery, R., Nihar, A., White, G. R. T., & Madichie, N. O. (2020b). Keeping it in the family: Exploring Igbo ethnic entrepreneurial behaviour in Nigeria. *International Journal of Entrepreneurial Behavior & Research*, 26(1), 34–53.

Igwe, P. A., Okolie, U. C., & Nwokoro, C. V. (2019). Towards a responsible entrepreneurship education and the future of the workforce. *The International Journal of Management Education*, 100300. doi:10.1016/j.ijme.2019.05.001

Imhonopi, D., Urim, U. M., Kasumu, T. O., & Onwumah, A. (2016). Dehexing women entrepreneurship in Nigeria: Turning possibilities into realities. *Gender & Behaviour*, 14(3), 7855–7881.

International Fund for Agricultural Development [IFAD]. (2004). *Enhancing the role of indigenous women in sustainable development: IFAD experience with indigenous women in Latin America and Asia*. Third Session of the Permanent Forum on Indigenous Issues, Italy.

Jennings, J. E., & Brush, C. G. (2013). Research on women entrepreneurs: Challenges to (and from) the broader entrepreneurship literature? *The Academy of Management Annals*, 7(1), 663–715.

Kimmitta, J., Munozb, P., & Newbery, R. (2019). Poverty and the varieties of entrepreneurship in the pursuit of prosperity. *Journal of Business Venturing*, 34(4), 646–663.

Lincoln, Y., & Guba, E. G. (1985). *Naturalistic inquiry*. Newbury Park. CA: Sage.

Madichie, N. O. (2011). Setting an agenda for women entrepreneurship in Nigeria: A commentary on Faseke's journey through time for The Nigerian woman. *Gender in Management*, 26(3), 212–219.

Madichie, N. O., Nkamnebe, A. D., & Ekanem, I. U. (2020). Marketing in the informal economy: An entrepreneurial perspective and research agenda. In *Entrepreneurship marketing: Principles and practice of SME marketing* (pp. 412–428). UK: Routledge.

Matthews, C. H., & Moser, S. B. (1996). A longitudinal investigation of the impact of family background. *Journal of Small Business Management*, 34(2), 29–43.

Meagher, K. (2010). *Identity economics: Social networks and the informal economy in Nigeria*. Suffolk, UK: James Currey. Retrieved from http://eprints.lse.ac.uk/id/eprint/27379

Minniti, M. (2010). Female entrepreneurship and economic activity. *The European Journal of Development Research*, 22(3), 294–312.

Murphy, P. J., & Coombes, S. M. (2009). A model of social entrepreneurial discovery. *Journal of Business Ethics*, 87(3), 325–336.

Nnadozie, E. (2002). African indigenous entrepreneurship determinants of resurgence and growth of Igbo entrepreneurship during the post-biafra period. *Journal of African Business*, 3(1), 49–80.

Obunike, C. L. (2016). Induction strategies of Igbo entrepreneurs and micro-business success: A study of household equipment line, main market, Onitsha, Nigeria. *Economics and Business*, 4, 43–65.

Okolie, U. C., Nwosu, H. E., & Mlanga, S. (2019). Graduate employability: How the higher education institutions can meet the demand of the labour market. *Higher Education, Skills and Work-based Learning*, 9(4), 620–636.

Olulu, R. M., & Udeora, S. A. (2018). Contract of apprenticeship and employment generation in Nigeria. *International Journal of Scientific Research in Education*, 11(3), 335–344.

Oregiu, J. J., & Nafiu, A. T. (2014). An exploratory study of Igbo entrepreneurial activity and business success in Nigeria as the panacea for economic growth and development. *International Journal of Scientific & Technology Research*, 3(9), 158–165.

Ortiz-Ospina, E., & Roser, M. (2016). *World poverty*. Retrieved from https://ourworldindata.org/world-poverty

Peredo, A. M., & Chrisman, J.J. (2006). Toward a theory of community-based enterprise. *The Academy of Management Review*, 31(2), 309–328.

Peredo, A. M., Anderson, R. B., Galbraith, C., Honig, B., & Dana, L. P. (2004). Towards a theory of indigenous entrepreneurship. *International Journal of Entrepreneurship and Small Business, 1*(1), 1–19.

Ratten, V., & Dana, L. (2017). Gendered perspective of indigenous entrepreneurship. *Small Enterprise Research, 24*(1), 62–72.

Sen, A. K. (1999). *Development as freedom.* New York: Knopf.

Shah, H., & Saurabh, P. (2015). Women entrepreneurs in developing nations: Growth and replication strategies and their impact on poverty alleviation. *Technology Innovation Management Review, 5*(8), 34–43.

Shepherd, D. A., Parida, V., & Wincent, J. (2020). Entrepreneurship and poverty alleviation: The importance of health and children's education for slum entrepreneurs. *Entrepreneurship Theory and Practice*, 1–35. doi:10.1177/1042258719900774

Sutter, C., Bruton, G. D., & Chen, J. (2019). Entrepreneurship as a solution to extreme poverty: A review and future research directions. *Journal of Vocational Venturing, 34*, 197–214.

Todd, R. (2012). Young urban Aboriginal women entrepreneurs: Social capital, complex transitions and community support. *British Journal of Canadian Studies, 25*(1), 1–19.

Uduku, O. (2002). The socio-economic basis of a diaspora community: *Igbo-bu-Ike. Review of African Political Economy, 29*(92), 301–311.

Unruh, J., Adewusi, A., & Boolaky, M. (2014). The impact of gender difference on entrepreneurship inclinations in Nigeria. *International Journal of Business and Globalisation, 13*(1), 1–24.

Vollstedt, M., & Rezat, S. (2019). An introduction to grounded theory with a special focus on axial coding and the coding paradigm. In Kaiser & N. Presmeg (Eds.), *Compendium for Early Career Researchers in Mathematics Education, pp. 81–100.* ICME-13 Monographs, Switzerland. doi:10.1007/978-3-030-15636-7_4

Wilson, T. D., Gámez Vázquez, A. E., & Ivanova, A. (2012). Women Beach and Marina Vendors in Cabo San Lucas, Mexico: Consideration about their Marginalisation. *Latin American Perspectives, 39*(6), 83–95.

Winn, J. (2005). Women entrepreneurs: Can we remove the barriers? *International Entrepreneurship and Management Journal, 1*(1), 381–397.

Wood, G. J., & Davidson, M. J. (2011). A review of male and female australian indigenous entrepreneurs: Disadvantaged past-promising future? *Gender in Management: An International Journal, 26*(4), 311–326.

World, Bank (2020). Nigeria releases new report on poverty and inequality in country. Retrieved from https://www.worldbank.org/en/programs/lsms/brief/nigeria-releases-new-report-on-poverty-and-inequality-in-country.

Entrepreneurial Competencies and the Performance of Informal SMEs: The Contingent Role of Business Environment

Ayodotun Stephen Ibidunni, Oyedele Martins Ogundana [iD] and Arinze Okonkwo

ABSTRACT

This study examined entrepreneurial competencies as a viable pathway for improving the innovative performance of SMEs in Nigeria's informal sector and the contingent roles of the business environment. A survey research design was used to gather data from 296 entrepreneurs who operate informal SMEs in Nigeria. Based on the findings from the SEM-PLS multivariate analysis, the study concluded that entrepreneurial competencies, especially organizing, conceptual, learning, strategic, opportunity, and risk-taking competencies, are essential for achieving higher innovation performance. The study also reveals that entrepreneurial competencies are useful toward mitigating environmental pressures resulting from operational turbulence and erratic policy changes, as the firm drives toward improving innovation outputs. As such, the entrepreneurship environment is becoming more endogenous as entrepreneurs, through their entrepreneurial competencies, have started to gain control over it. This study contributes to the entrepreneurship literature by highlighting the most essential competencies alongside the relevant contingencies. By doing that, this study offers a practical guide on priority competence area that entrepreneurship stakeholders, including entrepreneurs and policymakers, should consider for investment.

1. Introduction

Across the globe, small and medium enterprises (SMEs) make enormous contributions toward economic growth and active engagement of citizens. The assertion is as much real with the developing economies as it is with the developed economies (Ogundana, 2020b). OECD (2018) opined that SMEs embody about a totality of global businesses, accounting for about 70% of all employments and generating an average range of 50% to 60% of value-added. In Africa, SMEs support economic growth through job creation in different sectors of endeavors, improve means of livelihood, industrial production upturn, and export, social enrichment as well as governmental constancy and they serve as a mainstream revenue generation in many of these economies, including in Nigeria (Ifekwem & Adedamola, 2016; Ogundana, Galanakis, Simba, & Oxborrow, 2018b;

Shehnaz & Ramayah, 2015). However, they also must deal with challenges that pertain to sustaining their performance and continuity. For example, the informality of the substantial African SMEs industry poses a problem as to multiple taxations, unaccountable levies, and little government support on the SMEs industry. With particular emphasis on Nigeria which has the largest population of persons in the African continent and a dominant SMEs industry of over forty-one million businesses (SMEDAN, 2017), there is no doubt that the SMEs industry occupies a strategic position within the nation's business hub (Ogundana, Galanakis, Simba, & Oxborrow, 2018a). However, this present study is particular about two critical issues that relate to SMEs in Nigeria. The first issue relates to the fact that the informal nature of the SMEs industry in Nigeria, with little regulations and support from the Government, leaves the industry operators to secure their means to business survival and growth (Ingenbleek, 2019; Madichie, Mpofu, & Kolo, 2017). Consequently, firms in the Nigerian SMEs sector are poised to engage higher levels of their respective entrepreneurial competencies in combating the challenges of securing funds, competing with their foreign counterparts and with other large firms in related industries (Jevwegaga et al., 2018).

In other to deal with SMEs coping capabilities with these challenges, entrepreneurial competencies appear to be a viable tool to engage (Zizile & Tendai, 2018). Entrepreneurial competencies are the capabilities that entrepreneurs develop and inculcate into their firms' cultural patterns of operations in order to sustain performance and improve their competitive positions in the industry. According to Gwadabe and Amirah (2017), in recent times, business activities have become more competitive, and this has increased the failure of SMEs in Nigeria due to the environment and the increased competition. Entrepreneurial competencies have become very important to the survival of SMEs in Nigeria. Entrepreneurial competencies are vital to the achievement of competitive advantage in business through different measures, like proper management of relationships (Shehnaz & Ramayah, 2015). Concerning innovative performance, entrepreneurial competencies facilitate entrepreneurs' capability to identify industry opportunities, exploit collaborative platforms across industrial sectors, and define a suitable pathway for the future success of the firm (Ibidunni, Olokundun, Oke, & Nwaomonoh, 2017a). According to Zizile and Tendai (2018), the survival and success of SME have been positively affected by entrepreneurial competencies; they also serve as critical aids in the achievement of innovation performance among SMEs. A recent study by Gümüsay and Bohné (2018) affirmed that entrepreneurial competencies also help in the judicious and appropriate allocation of a firm's scarce resources which generally aims at the attainment of an organization's goals and objectives which reflects in its overall performance. In light of this, entrepreneurial competencies as a form of internally induced SMEs growth mechanism is a practical interventionist pathway to enhancing SMEs innovativeness (Gwadabe & Amirah, 2017). However, there has been very little empirical evidence in the literature to support entrepreneurial competencies as an interventionist strategy of the informal sector SMEs in Nigeria, in achieving innovation performance. Thus, this study poses a question about what interventionist role(s) do entrepreneurial competencies have on the innovation performance of informal SMEs in Nigeria?

The second issue which the present study seeks to investigate relates to the contingent role of the business environment in which informal sector SMEs operate and attempt to develop competencies for innovation. Prior studies have established that the business environment is critical to the performance of SMEs (Ibidunni, Kolawole, et al., 2020; Ogundana, Galanakis, Simba, & Oxborrow, 2019; Uzairu & Noor, 2017). For example, Abiodun and Ibidunni (2014), Ibidunni et al. (2017a), and Weerakoon and Kodithuwakku (2018) argued that entrepreneurial competencies consist of internal environmental capabilities of the firm for sustaining performance. However, the influence of the business environment, especially the external environment, on innovation performance of SMEs appear to have received very little research attention in the literature, especially as it relates with developing economies like Nigeria. Nevertheless, this relationship is critical to such economies like Nigeria, where high levels of political instability and erratic policies are making the ease of doing business along forgone adventure (Adeeko, 2017; Damilola, Deborah, Oyedele, & Kehinde, 2020).

Moreover, this discursive omission from the literature limits the generalization of entrepreneurial competencies theory, especially given the conditions surrounding, therefore mentioned peculiarities of developing nations. Consequently, this study aims to fill this research gap by examining the relationship between entrepreneurial competencies, business environment, and innovation performance of informal SMEs in Nigeria. Upon these two established premises, this study's objective is to investigate entrepreneurial competencies as a viable pathway for improving the innovative performance of SMEs in Nigeria's informal sector and the contingent roles of business environment on that relationship. The next section of this work discusses the theoretical background and hypotheses that this study investigated. The third section is the methodology, and it will be followed by the analyses section, which depicts the statistical strength of the current study. After this, in the fifth section, the discussion section will elaborate on the findings of this study in relation to previous studies. Lastly, the fifth and sixth sections will show the practical and theoretical implications of this study, and the conclusion and further studies, respectively.

2. Literature review

2.1. Informal SMEs

The informal Small and Medium-scale Enterprises (SMEs) refer to any enterprise that is not fully regulated by the Government and other public authorities (Fapohunda, 2012; Saidu & Dauda, 2014). This includes enterprises that are not officially registered and do not maintain a complete set of accounts (Bank of Industry, 2018). They include and are not limited to street traders, subsistence farmers, small-scale manufacturers, and service providers including hairdressers, private taxi drivers, and carpenters (Fajana, 2008; Fapohunda, 2012). Most informal SMEs often operate without a structure, underground, subterranean, and unabsorbed (Ikadeh & Cloete, 2020; Saidu & Dauda, 2014). However, they continue to thrive in all economies, including the developing and industrialized countries, as they currently account for about half of global employment (International Labor Organization, 2002). According to the International Monetary Fund (IMF, 2019), the informal sector accounts for approximately 72% of the workforce in sub-Saharan Africa, excluding agriculture. In Nigeria, the Bank of Industry (BOI, 2018) stated that informal SMEs account for more than 65% of Nigeria's 2017 GDP representing a 24% increase from the 2016 GDP contribution. In addition to that, the Nigerian informal SMEs contribute 57.9% of Nigeria's GNP at 212.6 USD billion (Akintimehin et al., 2019).

Informal SMEs also contribute to the reduction in the level of unemployment by employing over 48 million Nigerians (Akintimehin et al., 2019; Asalaye, Popoola, Lawal, Ogundipe, & Ezenwoke, 2018). Many entrepreneurs have utilized the informal sector as a stepping-stone into formality (Asalaye et al., 2018). Others have used it to work their way out of poverty (ILO, 2002). The flexibility of the informal economies enabled many who are gainfully employed in the formal economies to create additional revenue, popularly known as "side-hustle in Nigeria (Akintimehin et al., 2019). However, many other economic benefits derivable from the informal enterprise activities are still unknown, mainly because the sector is highly dynamic (Saidu & Dauda, 2014). As such, the Nigerian Government continue to introduce policy interventions to improve the productivity of informal sector players (BOI, 2018). For instance, the Nigerian Government introduced the Government Economic Empowerment Programme (GEEP) and Artisanal and Small-Scale Miners – "ASM Fund" to provide both training and financial supports to market women, artisans, and traders. The Nigerian Government also introduced the N-Power programme, a skill empowerment programme designed to help Nigerian entrepreneurs to acquire and develop life-long skills and competencies (National Social Investments Programme, 2020). Despite the introduction of different training and reskilling programmes, it is not clear whether those competencies could improve the performances of informal SMEs. This knowledge is crucial to improve the economic benefits derivable from the informal sector.

2.2. Entrepreneurial competencies

The concept of entrepreneurial competencies has its foundation not only in the competency and competence literature but also in the literature of entrepreneurship. Unfortunately, the definitions of entrepreneurial competencies are still elusive within the field of entrepreneurship (Mitchelmore & Rowley, 2010). Nonetheless, the phenomenon is primarily described as a group of competencies that enable and support successful entrepreneurship (Madichie, 2009; Man, Lau, & Chan, 2002; Thomas & Herrisier, 1991). There is a consensus that those group of competencies, required for successful entrepreneurship, are embodied within an entrepreneur who adds value through organizing resources and opportunities for their businesses (Bird, 2019). Of further importance is that the entrepreneurial competencies are learnable; therefore, recognizing the importance of competencies and identifying that it is crucial for educators and the development of learning opportunities (Mitchelmore & Rowley, 2010). It is suggested in the literature that entrepreneurial competencies are associated with the lifecycle of organizations (Chandler & Hanks, 1994; Chandler & Jansen, 1992; Johnson & Winterton, 1999). Scholars opined that entrepreneurial competencies are needed mainly to operate small or new businesses (Colombo & Grilli, 2005; Man et al., 2002). Thus, Bird (1995) described entrepreneurial competencies as "baseline competencies" which are necessary to plan or launch a new venture. On the other hand, scholars (such as Bird, 1995; Johnson & Winterton, 1999; Man et al., 2002) believed that entrepreneurs require managerial competencies to operate and grow large organizations. It is this theoretical assumption that underlines our study of entrepreneurial competence in informal SMEs which are often small in their sizes.

Individually, scholars have described entrepreneurial competencies in similar but diverse ways. Bird (1995) described it as underlying characteristics such as specific knowledge, motives, traits, self-images, social roles and skills which result in venture birth, survival and growth. Man et al. (2002) defined entrepreneurial competencies as the total ability of the entrepreneur to perform a job role successfully. In a study conducted by Bartlett and Ghoshal (1997), three categories of competencies, attitudes/traits, knowledge/experience, and, skills/abilities, were identified. Stuart and Lindsay (1997) similarly also defined entrepreneurial competencies as a person's skills, knowledge, and personal characteristics. Entrepreneurial competencies have also been understood in terms of traits, skills and knowledge (Ibidunni, Ogunnaike, & Abiodun, 2017; Man, Lau, & Snape, 2008). Baum, Locke, and Smith (2001) formed a list of nine entrepreneurial competencies based on the work of others (Chandler & Jansen, 1992); these were knowledge, cognitive ability, self-management, administration, human resource, decision skill, leadership, opportunity recognition, opportunity development, and organization skill. Man (2001) identified the following ten areas of entrepreneurial competencies: opportunity, relationship, analytical, innovative, operational, human, strategic, commitment, learning, and personal strength competencies. Mitchelmore and Rowley (2010) described entrepreneurial competencies as the identification and definition of a viable market niche, the development of products/services, idea generation, environmental scanning, and exploiting opportunities.

One of the reasons behind the unaligned definitions is enshrined in the different underpinning assumptions utilized by various researchers in arriving at their perception of entrepreneurial competence. Chandler and Jansen (1992) adopted a similar approach, explicitly taking an antecedent perspective by attempting to delineate fundamental knowledge or abilities thought to reflect their understanding of entrepreneurial competencies. Mitchell et al. (2002) and Shepherd (1999) commonly utilized a process or behavioral approach to studying entrepreneurial competencies in order to be in line with the process dimension of the competitiveness condition. This approach assumes that the mere possession of competencies does not necessarily make an entrepreneur competent. Instead, competencies can only be demonstrated by a person's behavior and actions, which correspond to the dynamism characteristic of competitiveness (Man et al., 2002). Finally, other researchers, such as Lerner and Almor (2002), chose a performance-based perspective by identifying essential tasks and then assessing skill acumen; the assessments were subjective self-perceptions. In summary, over the last two decades, there have been several investigations in different contexts that have sought to generate lists of entrepreneurial competencies, with varying levels of categorization (for example, Man et al., 2002; Bartlett & Ghoshal, 1997; Baum, 1994; Bird, 1995; Chandler & Jansen, 1992). Some researchers have used alternative terms such as skills or expertise, but their research generates findings that are relevant to the general field of entrepreneurial competencies.

2.3. *Entrepreneurial competencies and business performance*

Resource-based theorists have noted that entrepreneurs and their competencies are a critical and valuable resource of the firms (Barney, 1991; Grant, 1991). Bird (1995) suggests that since competency refers to the quality of action taken by entrepreneurs; it is directly related to venture outcomes. However, the conclusions of prior studies have been mostly inconsistent with regards to what particular form of entrepreneurial competence influences the performance of businesses. Chandler and Jansen (1992) operationalize founder competencies identified in the literature and cluster these according to three fundamental roles, traditional entrepreneurial skills; the managerial role and technical-functional role. Their results revealed that self-reported competencies of founders were correlated with venture performance. In a study conducted by Man et al. (2002), the six aspects of entrepreneurial competencies had either direct or indirect impacts on SME performance. The results of Baum's (1994) study show that self-efficacy, technical skill, personal marketing, innovation/production focus, and passion for work had the most robust direct positive relationships with venture growth. However, Baum (1994) observed that other aspects of entrepreneurial experiences such as vision, organization skill, growth goals, opportunity skill and industry experience had a less positive influence on business performance. Fabrizio, Paolo, and Alessandra (2011) examined the influence of entrepreneurial competencies on the business performance of small and medium-sized Italian firms. The results of their study showed that dimensions of entrepreneurial competencies, including efficiency orientation, planning, persuasiveness, self-confidence, organizational awareness, teamwork, and leadership, yielded an improved output of firm performance.

An American study by Hood and Young (1993) to develop a theoretical framework of successful entrepreneurs questioned 100 leading entrepreneurs and chief executive officers of America's fastest-growing entrepreneurial firms. Hood and Young (1993) identified that the entrepreneurial competencies that were most important were leadership skills, closely followed by human relations skills, oral communications skills, and written communications skills. However, the other forms of entrepreneurial competencies (including management skills, deal-making skills, logical thinking, analytical skills, decision-making skills, goal setting skills, hiring skills, and business plan preparation) had little or no significant influence on business performance. Aruni, Akira, and Hironori (2014) investigated the impact of entrepreneurial competencies on entrepreneurial orientation of manufacturing firms in Sri Lanka. Their study included one hundred and nine (109) owner/managers in the private sector tea factories. Aruni et al. (2014) observed that entrepreneurs' strategic and commitment competencies directly relate with to entrepreneurial orientation. It is evident from the foregoing discussions that the aspects of entrepreneurial competencies that influence the performance of businesses are inconsistent. Additionally, it is unclear what aspects of entrepreneurial competencies will influence the performances of informal SMEs in a developing country context. The focus on the developing region is incredibly crucial, especially as existing studies are primarily from the developed country context. Welter (2011) and Madichie, Hinson, and Ibrahim (2013) observed that the developing country context would differ from the context of a developed country because of their unique spatial, institutional, and social contexts. It is this focus that drives this study.

Consequently, this present study hypothesizes that:

H1: Within a developing economy context of informal entrepreneurs, conceptual entrepreneurial competencies directly and positively support the innovation performance of SMEs

H2: Within a developing economy context of informal entrepreneurs, learning entrepreneurial competencies directly and positively supports the innovation performance of SMEs

H3: Within a developing economy context of informal entrepreneurs, risk-taking entrepreneurial competencies directly and positively supports the innovation performance of SMEs

H4: Within a developing economy context of informal entrepreneurs, strategic entrepreneurial competencies directly and positively support the innovation performance of SMEs

H5: Within a developing economy context of informal entrepreneurs, relationship entrepreneurial competencies directly and positively support the innovation performance of SMEs

H6: Within a developing economy context of informal entrepreneurs, opportunity entrepreneurial competencies directly and positively support the innovation performance of SMEs

2.4. Entrepreneurial competencies and environmental complexity

Ibidunni and Ogundele (2013) identified the business environment to be dynamic and unstable; this indicated the complexity of the business environment. The performance of entrepreneurs also depends on the external environment, which is not within the control of the entrepreneur (Adeeko, 2017). The above stated supports the notion that environmental factors are very much uncontrollable by the entrepreneur, and this has led to complexity in the environment, which most times translates to business failure. The external environment also consists of government policies, laws, insecurity, corruption, infrastructure, financial support, and culture (White, 2004), all these factors affect the performance of SMEs especially in a country like Nigeria which is unstable politically and economically. Obiwuru, Oluwalaiye, and Okwu (2011) in their study appraised the intrinsic and extrinsic (internal and external) environment of Nigerian businesses through the SWOT and PESTEL models and deduced that the external environment which is the complex environment is more related to Strategic management. Ibidunni et al. (2017a) defined strategic competencies as the ability of an entrepreneur to carry out business activities properly. In addition to that, they also mentioned that most businesses that fail, fail because of their inability of the entrepreneur to plan and envisage their complex environment strategically.

H7: The relationship between entrepreneurial competencies and the innovation performance of informal entrepreneurs in developing economies can be strengthened by the capacity to manage environmental complexity

2.5. Entrepreneurial competencies and environmental dynamism

Environmental dynamism can be the way choices and preferences of consumers change from time to time (Wijbenga and Van Witteloostuijn 2007). This also aids SMEs in creating a structure which in turn affects performance (Miles, Covin, & Heeley, 2000). Government policies benefit developed countries more than other developing and under-developed nations (Cadbury World, 2014; Fitzgerald, 2005) which spoke how the Cadbury brand demolished the French monopoly in the cocoa industry through the effective government policy adopted by the United Kingdom back in the mid-1850s. This also resulted in massive sales growth and publicity. To further support the above stated, reports in the Global Entrepreneurship and Development Institute (Acs, Szerb & Autio, 2015) stated that the USA ranked as the highest nation that supports SMEs with funds, expansion schemes, and policies. Also, Canada and Australia came second and third, respectively. All these countries are highly developed, and the economies continue to thrive due to the deliberate effort made by the countries to booster entrepreneurial activities in their home nations. Obaji and Olugu (2014) reckoned in their study that strategic management is essential in the study, and strategic management still translates to strategic skills and abilities. This is aimed at helping the entrepreneur plan properly and plan beyond the foreseeable future.

H8: The relationship between entrepreneurial competencies and the innovation performance of informal entrepreneurs in developing economies is strengthened by the capacity to manage environmental dynamism

3. Methodology

The present study adopted a survey research method for investigating the moderating impact of business environment on the relationship of entrepreneurial competencies and innovation performance of SMEs in Nigeria's informal sector. In this research work, the research subjects are SMEs in Alaba International market. The estimated population of small and medium enterprises in Alaba International market amounts to 50,000 (Christian, 2019). In this particular research, the Bartlett, Kotrlik, and Higgins (2001) formula was used to determine the sample size. This estimation, with an alpha value of 0.05 produced a sample size of 370 respondents for this study. However, 296 (80%) copies of distributed copies of the questionnaire were retrieved and valid for inclusion in this research. Table 1 shows the respondents demographic information for this study. Table 1 shows the demographic data of respondents.

Table 1 shows that 178 (60.1%) of respondents are male, and 118 (39.9%) of the sample study are female. Table 1 also shows the age distribution of respondents of the demographic. Fourteen (4.7%) of the respondents are between the age range of below 20 years, 134 (45.3%) of the respondents are between 21 and 30 years, 118 (39.9%) of respondents are between the age range 31–40 years, and 30 (10.1%) of the respondents are of the age category of 40 years and above. The education qualification distribution within Table 1 shows that 79 (26.7%) had WASSCE/O LEVEL, 53 (17.9%) had NCE/OND, 143 (48.3%) had HDND/B.SC while 21 (7.1%) is Post Graduate. Thus, implying that respondents of diverse educational backgrounds participated in this research, but HND/BSc holder is the

Table 1. Demographic Data of Respondents.

		Frequency	Per cent
Entrepreneurs' Biodata			
Gender	Male	178	60.1
	Female	118	39.9
	Total	**296**	**100.0**
Age	Below 20 years	14	4.7
	21–30 years	134	45.3
	31–40 years	118	39.9
	40 – years & above	30	10.1
	Total	**296**	**100.0**
Educational Qualification	WASSCE/O LEVEL	79	26.7
	NCE/OND	53	17.9
	HND/B.SC	143	48.3
	POSTGRADUATE MBA	21	7.1
	Total	**296**	**100.0**
Firms' Biodata			
Year Company Started Operation	Below 5 years	14	4.7
	5–10 years	79	26.7
	10 years & above	202	68.2
	Total	**296**	**100.0**
Number of Employees	Less than 10	144	48.6
	10–49	152	51.4
	Total	**296**	**100.0**

Source: Authors' Idea.

significant respondents. Concerning the firm-level demographic data, Table 1 reveals that 14 (4.7%) of the SMEs fall under the category below 5 years, 79 (26.7%) of the firms are 5–10 years, while 202 (68.2%) firms are 10 years and above of existence. Table 1 also shows the number of staff working with the firms to include 144 (48.6%) SMEs have less than 10 staffs, while 152 (51.4%) of the firms have between 10 and 49 staff. Thus, the respondents spread for this study typically occupy the categories of micro and small firms. This data conforms typically to the complete spread dominance of micro and small firms in the Nigerian SMEs industry (SMEDAN, 2017).

3.1. Measures

The items in this study adapted from existing studies. Each item used a 5-point Likert scale (1 = *strongly disagree*, 5 = *strongly* agree). Table 1 shows all items and their respective factor loading. Entrepreneurial competencies were measured by Man et al. (2002) and Ahmad, Ramayah, Wilson, and Kummerow (2010). It measured the extent to which entrepreneurs that are SME operators in Nigeria's informal technology-based market demonstrate organizing, conceptual, learning, risk-taking, strategic, relationship, and opportunity competencies in carrying out their businesses. During the assessment of measures for this study, some items relating to organizing, relationship, and opportunity competencies were removed because of weak loading, while other items were retained. Innovation performance was measured using the scale as developed by Kesinro, Adenugba, and Ademilua (2018); Ibidunni, Iyiola, and Ibidunni (2014), and is comprised of six items that measured the extent to which the SMEs entrepreneurs sustain an innovation culture in their firms and in fulfilling customers' expectations. The moderating variable business environment as measured by Jansen, Van Den Bosch, and Volberda (2006), and Gaganis, Pasiouras, and Voulgari (2019). This scale consisted of two dimensions, namely, environmental complexity and environmental dynamism. Environmental complexity scale comprised three items related to the extent to which the informal sector entrepreneurs perceived their operating environment to be highly competitive and turbulent. On the other hand, the environmental dynamism scale comprised three items that measured the extent to which the entrepreneurs perceived their industry environment to be unpredictable, highly characterized by change and volatile as a result of customers' changing tastes and competitors' operational dynamism.

3.2. Measurement assessment

To ensure the construct validity of the research scales, this study explored the various items of entrepreneurial competencies to ensure their consistency with previously established scales (for example, Ahmad et al., 2010; Man et al., 2002). Factor analysis was used to examine the exploratory factor analysis (EFA) (see Table 2) to identify whether the items loading corresponded with the factors intended. Seven distinct factors emerged, namely, organizing competency, conceptual competency, learning competency, risk-taking competency, strategic competency, relationship competency, and opportunity competency. Items that had loading lower than 0.5 were removed. The retained items all had factor loadings ranging from 0.5 to 0.933; hence, considered to be significant (Hair, Anderson, Tatham, & Black, 1998). In order to ensure the confirmatory factor analysis (CFA) of the scale, the study used the measurement scale provision of smart PLS (See Figure 1). The outer loading of all the factors representing entrepreneurial competencies was significant at $p < 0.05$ level of statistical significance.

Similarly, the overall outputs of the innovation performance scale reflected that factors were significant at $p < 0.05$ level of statistical significance. To examine the reliability and convergence validity of the scales, this study computed Cronbach alpha statistics and the composite reliability (CR) for each measure. Generally, the Cronbach's alpha values were within the 0.7 boundaries or greater, while the CR values were greater than 0.7; hence, indicating supporting the reliability and convergence validity of all the scales (Bagozzi & Yi, 1988). Also, the study further assessed validity by computing the average variance explained (AVE). Holistically, the AVE values for the scales revolved around 0.5 and greater for all the measures (Hair, Risher, Sarstedt, & Ringle, 2019). This study further evaluated discriminant validity by adopting Fornell and Larcker (1981) recommendation that the correlation between measures must not exceed the square root of AVE. The values in Table 3 depict the correlation matric of all the scales for this study, and it ascertained that Fornell and Larcker's recommendation was achieved. Hence, discriminant validity for the scale is assured.

4. Analysis

This study made use of Smart PLS to test for the hypotheses earlier raised. The statistical significance of the respective regression coefficient (beta) in the structural model was specified with their accompanying P-values. P-values that were below 0.5 were considered to be statistically significant in this study. Hence, the test of hypotheses ensured that the P-values accompanying each beta coefficient were examined for significance.

Figure 1 shows the multivariate analysis result for this current study using SmartPLS. The focus of this study was to investigate the moderating impact of business environment on the relationship of entrepreneurial competencies and innovation performance of

Table 2. Exploratory Factor Analysis.

Item	1	2	3	4	5	6	7	8	9	10
Organizing Competency (Cronbach's alpha: 0.832, CR: 0.894, AVE: 0.685)										
ability to keep the organization running smoothly	.684									
ability to organize resources	.857									
....ability to coordinate tasks*	.409									
ability to identify my own strengths and weaknesses and match them with opportunities and threats	.854									
ability to learn proactively	.702									
Conceptual Competency (Cronbach's alpha: 0.764, CR: 0.820, AVE: 0.448)										
....ability to treat new problems as opportunities		.595								
ability to integrate ideas, issues, and observation into more general contexts		.691								
ability to monitor progress toward objectives in risky actions		.795								
ability to identify goods or services customers want		.613								
ability to actively look for products and services that provide real benefit to customers		.605								
ability to redesign the department and organization to meet long-term objectives and changes better		.575								
Learning Competency (Cronbach's alpha: 0.755, CR: 0.844, AVE: 0.575)										
....ability to possess an extremely strong internal drive			.757							
ability to manage my career development			.596							
ability to recognize and work on my shortcomings			.586							
ability to learn as much as I can in my field			.800							
Risk-taking Competency (Cronbach's alpha: 0.705, CR: 0.812, AVE: 0.534)										
....capability to explore new ideas				.620						
ability to take reasonable job-related risks				.701						
ability to commit to long-term business goals				.581						
ability to learn from a variety of means				.808						
Strategic Competency (Cronbach's alpha: 0.755, CR: 0.884, AVE: 0.792)										
....ability to prioritize work in alignment with business goals					.785					
ability to refuse to let the venture fail whenever appropriate					.694					
Relationship Competency (Cronbach's alpha: 0.616, CR: 0.798, AVE: 0.576)										
....ability to develop long-term trusting relationships with others*						.476				
ability to perceive unmet customer needs						.531				
ability to lead subordinates						.617				
ability to organize people						.685				
Opportunity Competency (Cronbach's alpha: 0.690, CR: 0.793, AVE: 0.572)										
....desire to communicate with others effectively							.813			
ability to look at old problems in new ways							.667			
ability to align current actions with strategic goals*							.334			
ability to delegate effectively							.502			
Business Environment (Complexity) (Cronbach's alpha: 0.711, CR: 0.727, AVE: 0.699)										
competition in our local market is intense								.531		
the organizational unit has relatively strong competitors								.560		
changes in our local market are intense								.933		
Business Environment (Dynamism) (Cronbach's alpha: 0.638, CR: 0.774, AVE: 0.732)										
customers regularly ask for new products and services									.641	
volumes of products and services to be delivered change fast and often									.715	
competition in our local market is extremely high									.828	
Innovation Performance (Cronbach's alpha: 0.788, CR: 0.851, AVE: 0.491)										
innovation-based organization										.773
customers prefer us for our innovative services more than our competitors										.631
customers appreciate the quality of our services										.768

(*Continued*)

Table 2. (Continued).

Item	1	2	3	4	5	6	7	8	9	10
customers tend to look for new offerings at all times										.881
Provides meaningful changes in services that add value to customers' satisfaction.										.712
Work continuously to develop a relationship with our customers.										.702

Notes: Values in parentheses represent construct reliability (that is, Cronbach's alpha, Composite Reliability – CR, Average Variance Extracted – AVE).
*Indicates an item that was removed from the scale because of a weak loading.

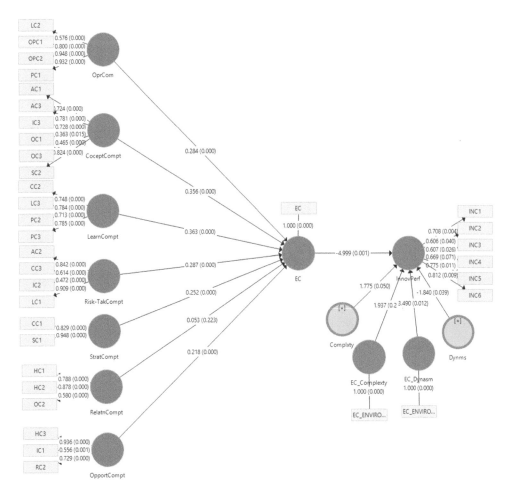

Figure 1. Structural Equation Model Showing Regression Weights (P-values). **Source**: Authors' Idea based on findings.

SMEs in Nigeria's informal sector. The study tested the following hypotheses: within a developing economy context of informal entrepreneurs i) organizing entrepreneurial competencies directly and positively supports innovation performance of technology-based SMEs (H1); ii) conceptual entrepreneurial competencies directly and positively supports innovation performance of technology-based SMEs (H2); iii) learning

Table 3. Descriptive Statistics and Correlations.

	Mean	SD	1	2	3	4	5	6	7	8	9	10
Organzn_Compt	4.8007	.34317	1									
Concptul_Compt	4.8339	.25655	.192**	1								
Learning_Compt	4.7323	.35040	.281**	-.011	1							
Risktakng_Compt	4.6985	.33396	.099	.106	-.010	1						
Strategc_Compt	4.6976	.56204	.187**	.209**	.024	-.113	1					
Relatnsp_Compt	4.7973	.27891	-.019	-.014	.241**	.191**	-.007	1				
Opportuny_Compt	4.8412	.27572	-.025	.185**	.088	.285**	-.114	.285**	1			
Entrp_Compt	4.7716	.16285	.541**	.455**	.479**	.404**	.542**	.431**	.400**	1		
EntrpCompt_N_EnvComplx	4.8228	.19211	.574**	.281**	.551**	.404**	.304**	.045	.140*	.719**	1	
EntrpCompt_N_EnvDync	4.8256	.18962	.583**	.142*	.661**	.278**	.398**	.260**	.194**	.799**	.790**	1

Notes: N = 296; SD: Standard Deviation.
** Correlation is significant at the 0.01 level (2-tailed). *. Correlation is significant at the 0.05 level (2-tailed).

entrepreneurial competencies directly and positively supports innovation performance of technology-based SMEs (H3); iv) risk-taking entrepreneurial competencies directly and positively supports innovation performance of technology-based SMEs (H4); v) strategic entrepreneurial competencies directly and positively support innovation performance of technology-based SMEs (H5); vi) relationship entrepreneurial competencies directly and positively support innovation performance of technology-based SMEs (H6); vii) opportunity entrepreneurial competencies directly and positively support the innovation performance of technology-based SMEs (H7). The following moderating effects were also tested; viii) the relationship between entrepreneurial competencies and the innovation performance of informal entrepreneurs in developing economies is strengthened by the capacity to manage environmental complexity (H8); ix) the relationship between entrepreneurial competencies and the innovation performance of informal entrepreneurs in developing economies is strengthened by the capacity to manage environmental dynamism (H9). The results in Figure 1 show that organizing competence ($\beta = 0.244$, $P = 0.000$), conceptual competence ($\beta = 0.356$, $P = 0.000$), learning competence ($\beta = 0.363$, $P = 0.000$), risk-taking competence ($\beta = 0.287$, $P = 0.000$), strategic competence ($\beta = 0.252$, $P = 0.000$) and opportunity competence ($\beta = 0.218$, $P = 0.000$) all had significant positive and direct impacts on innovation performance. However, the impact of relationships competence ($\beta = 0.053$, $P = 0.223$) on innovation performance was not statistically significant. Besides, the results showed that environmental complexity ($\beta = 1.937$, $P = 0.214$) did not moderate the relationship between entrepreneurial competencies and innovation performance. On the other hand, environmental dynamism ($\beta = 3.490$, $P = 0.012$) was positioned as a contingent factor that enhances environmental competencies in achieving higher levels of innovation performance.

Table 4 shows the path coefficient of the research variables for the current study. As earlier mentioned, the significant levels among the entrepreneurial competencies and the business environment variables represented their significant impact on innovation performance. As shown in the table, the indicators that show a significant relationship among variables are significant at $P < 0.05$. The T-value is within the range of 1.220 to 8.808 at a confidence interval of 1.96.

The study further examined the statistical results to identify the effect sizes of each respective dimension of entrepreneurial orientation on innovation performance of MSMEs in the study context. This was done alongside the contingent variables, including environmental complexity and environmental dynamism. Figure 2 reflects the F-square (f2) values that show the effect size of each of the variables. According to Cohen (1988), effect sizes of f2 greater than or equal to 0.02 is small, f2 greater than or equal to 0.15 is medium, and f2 greater than or equal to 0.35 is large, respectively, for every relationship among variables. SMART PLS automatically calculates f2 analysis. Hence, the results in Figure 2 show that the competencies that matter most include conceptual competence (f2 = 1.700), learning competence (f2 = 1.512), risk-taking competence (f2 = 1.113), strategic competence (f2 = 0.922), organizing competence (f2 = 0.905), and opportunity competence (f2 = 0.637). This result indicates that relationship competence (f2 = 0.030) is not as effective as a predictor of entrepreneurial competencies. This indicates that most of the effect sizes of each dimension of entrepreneurial competencies are large. The effect size of the relationship between entrepreneurial competencies and innovation performance is large (f2 = 1.691). Also, the result shows that both dimensions of environmental

Table 4. Path Coefficients of the Research Variables.

	Original Sample (O)	Sample Mean (M)	Standard Deviation (STDEV)	T Statistics (O│/ST. DEV)	P Values
ConceptCompt -> EC	0.356	0.352	0.056	6.372	0.000
Complxty -> InnovPerf	1.775	1.955	0.904	1.964	0.050
Dynms -> InnovPerf	−1.840	−1.972	0.888	2.071	0.039
EC -> InnovPerf	−4.999	−4.798	1.512	3.305	0.001
EC_Complexty -> InnovPerf	1.937	1.628	1.556	1.245	0.214
EC_Dynasm -> InnovPerf	3.490	3.551	1.386	2.517	0.012
LearnCompt -> EC	0.363	0.355	0.041	8.808	0.000
OpportCompt -> EC	0.218	0.217	0.041	5.374	0.000
OrganizCompt -> EC	0.284	0.281	0.045	6.260	0.000
RelatnCompt -> EC	0.053	0.057	0.044	1.220	0.223
Risk-TakCompt -> EC	0.287	0.292	0.047	6.059	0.000
StratCompt -> EC	0.252	0.252	0.049	5.103	0.000

Source: Authors' Idea based on findings.

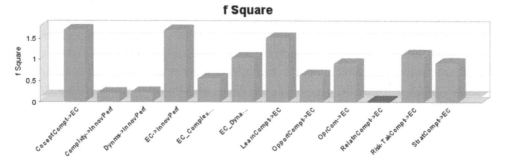

Figure 2. Effect Sizes of the Regression Relationships. **Source**: Authors' Idea based on findings.

complexity (f2 = 0.551) and environmental dynamism (f2 = 1.044) are effective moderators of entrepreneurial competencies and innovation performance.

5. Discussion

The outcomes of the present study supported the impact of entrepreneurial competencies on innovation performance of informal sector SMEs in the context studied. It also confirmed the moderating effect of business environment on entrepreneurial competencies and innovation performance. The study tested nine hypotheses in which the first seven hypotheses pertained to the direct impact of entrepreneurial competencies on innovation performance. Meanwhile, the eighth and ninth hypotheses investigated the moderating impacts on environmental complexity and environmental dynamism, respectively, on entrepreneurial competencies and innovation performance.

The results from the study revealed that six entrepreneurial competencies dimensions, namely organizing competence, conceptual competence, learning competence, risk-taking competence, strategic competence, and opportunity competence significantly related to innovation performance. This result is consistent with existing studies of Ahmad et al. (2010) that found a strong relationship between entrepreneurial competencies and business success in Malaysian SMEs. Within the context of spin-offs, Rasmussen, Mosey, and Wright (2011) observed that entrepreneurial competencies like championing, leveraging, and opportunity refinement support the capacity of the firms to gain credibility. On the other hand, our findings are inconsistent with that of Baum (1994) who concluded that entrepreneurial competencies (including vision, organization skill, growth goals, opportunity skill, and industry experience) have little or no influence on the performance of firms in the United States. Likewise, our findings are also inconsistent with Mitchelmore and Rowley (2010) who found that four clusters of entrepreneurial competences (including personal and relationship, business and management, entrepreneurial and human relations competencies) were less valuable to sampled entrepreneurs in England and Wales. Both inconsistencies are large because Baum's, Mitchelmore's and Rowley's measure of entrepreneurial competencies are different from that used in this current study. Most researchers acknowledge that entrepreneurial competence is a multidimensional construct whose definitions and measures are often divergent in the field of entrepreneurship (Man et al., 2002; Mitchelmore & Rowley, 2010). This implies that, because of the elusiveness of the phenomenon, it is difficult if not impossible, to conclude that entrepreneurial competence positively influences business performance. Instead, we are of the view that scholars should be relatively straightforward with regards to what aspect or measure of entrepreneurial competence that impacts or does not impact business performance.

Amongst the six entrepreneurial competencies examined, this present study found, in order of hierarchical arrangement, conceptual competence, learning competence, risk-taking competence, strategic competence, organizing competence, and opportunity competence to be a valuable support for Nigerian informal sector SMEs' drive for innovation performance. This present study suggests that theorists and practitioners that examine entrepreneurial competencies from a developing theory perspective, especially the present context should emphasize these set of competencies. Whereas this result is slightly consistent with existing studies, at the same time, it reflects some level of disparity with previous studies that were carried out in other developed and developing economies. For example, Ahmad et al. (2010) reported that opportunity recognition, capacity to act on opportunity, conceptual thinking, learning, and personal effectiveness are the entrepreneurial competencies that matter most in determining business success among Malaysian SMEs. Within the context of spin-offs, Rasmussen et al. (2011) observed that entrepreneurial competencies like championing, leveraging, and opportunity refinement support the capacity of the firms to gain credibility. Hence, given the peculiarity of the context of our study as a developing economy in which resource constraint challenges are a significant characteristic of the informal sector of MSMEs operations, our study makes a significant contribution, especially in the light of the unique prioritization of entrepreneurial competencies that we have suggested. However, our study finds some dimensional alignment with specific aspects of competencies that have been reported in previous studies. For example, Ibidunni, Mozie, and Ayeni (2020) found that the capacity of entrepreneurs in the informal sector to demonstrate risk-taking skills is an essential competency for driving innovation performance. This is, also, consistent with Covin and Slevin (1989), who observed that risk-taking competencies might cause small firms in hostile environments to exploit capital investments needed to develop or maintain a competitive edge. Likewise, risk-taking competence is critical in the Nigerian informal sector SMEs industry, primarily because of the need for entrepreneurs to survive in the business environment beyond all odds (Adegbuyi et al., 2018; Solesvik, 2012).

Quite surprisingly, our study did not support the direct impact of relationship competency on SMEs' innovation performance. This finding is contrary to existing studies like Man et al. (2008) that found the influence of relationship competencies on the long-term performance of SMEs given the interferences of competitive scope and organizational capabilities. The differential patterns of investigation between our study and existing studies may be reasons for mixed results in the findings of this present study compared to existing studies. Our study did not examine the competitive capabilities of the firm; instead, we focused the internal capacity of the firm to network with other firms in the industry, rather than to examine their collaborations amidst industry competitiveness. Hence, the impact of relationship competencies in SMEs cannot be under-emphasized depending on the perspective from which it is explained. This study revealed that the business environment is a contingent factor in determining the effectiveness of entrepreneurial competencies toward enhancing innovation performance of informal sector SMEs. The SMEs operators and policymakers can, therefore, focus on entrepreneurial development initiatives that pertain to the relevant aspects of individuals' skills and behavior. Specifically, the areas of interest include organizing, conceptual, learning, risk-taking, strategic, opportunity, and risk-taking competencies as essential dimensions of entrepreneurial competencies. The study also supported the moderating impact of environmental dynamism on entrepreneurial competencies and innovation performance. This result suggests that informal sector entrepreneurs in Nigeria who can complement their competencies with the changing business environment will achieve higher innovative performance. The finding of this study is consistent with Ahmad et al. (2010) that reported environmental dynamism as a contingent factor between entrepreneurial competencies and small business success. In addition to that, this study also revealed that entrepreneurial competencies are useful toward mitigating environmental pressures resulting from operational turbulence and erratic policy changes, as the firm drives toward improving innovation outputs. This result is inconsistent with Ogundana (in print). For instance, Ogundana (in print) described the Nigerian environment as exogenous where entrepreneurs have little or no control over it.

On the contrary, we observed that entrepreneurs within the Nigerian Informal SMEs could control their environments when they possess crucial entrepreneurial competence, including risk-taking competence. As such, we conclude that the Nigerian entrepreneurship environment is becoming more endogenous rather than exogenous. This means that Nigerian entrepreneurship can control and moderate the influence of their external environment through their entrepreneurial competence. Finally, there was evidence of an inverse moderating effect of environmental complexity on the relationship between entrepreneurial competencies and innovation performance of SMEs in Nigeria. This result from our study is consistent with previous studies like Baum et al. (2001) that established an almost insignificant effect of environmental complexity on venture growth of small firms. Meanwhile, Dolz, Iborra, and Safón (2018) affirmed that entrepreneurial ambidexterity is required for SMEs to cope within highly complex environments that are characterized by financial and economic crises. Hence, the findings from this recent study suggest that the capacity of SME operators in Nigeria to achieve innovation performance is not necessarily a function of high and low dimensions of environmental challenges. This may be evidenced by the fact that entrepreneurs, looking beyond external environmental interventions and shocks, strive within the confines of their limited resources to ensure the survival and resilience of their firms' operations.

6. Conclusion

In this study, the focus was to investigate entrepreneurial competencies as a viable pathway for improving the innovative performance of SMEs in Nigeria's informal sector and the contingent roles of business environment on that relationship. Based on the findings of the multivariate analysis, the study draws the conclusion that entrepreneurial competencies, especially organizing, conceptual, learning, risk-taking, strategic, opportunity, and risk-taking competencies are essential for achieving higher innovation performance. The study also suggests that entrepreneurial competencies are useful toward mitigating environmental pressures resulting from operational turbulence and erratic policy changes, as the firm drives toward improving innovation outputs. This study contributes to the entrepreneurial competence literature by highlighting the most critical competencies alongside the relevant contingencies. This is crucial, primarily as entrepreneurs operate within a resource-constrained environment. As such, this study provided a practical guide that will enable entrepreneurship stakeholders, including entrepreneurs and policymakers, to identify priority competence areas for investment. This study also contributes to the existing literature and theory on entrepreneurial competencies by investigating the role of entrepreneurial competencies within the context of the informal sector of an emerging economy. In our view, this is an essential contribution since the understanding of entrepreneurial competencies has been limited mainly to explaining entrepreneurial success within economies that operate within economies that are well regulated by government policies and laws. However, within informal sector economies of developing economies, the understanding of the interventionist perspective of entrepreneurial competencies in improving innovation performance of SMEs have been limited in the literature. Consequently, the adoption of exploratory factor analysis to examine what exact entrepreneurial competencies apply to the current context's informal sector gave insight to risk-taking competence as a novel and an essential dimension of entrepreneurial competency that support the innovation performance of SMEs.

The study also contributes to the strategic management and entrepreneurship literature on entrepreneurial competencies by providing insights about how firms in the informal sector can adopt intrinsic competencies within turbulent and dynamic environments to innovate and sustain performance. Also, the findings from this study provide a theoretical springboard for propelling further studies across the informal sector of developing economies that share similar characteristics with the current context under study. Establishing the theoretical fit of entrepreneurial competencies across a robust informal sector base of developing economies will supply insights about the roles of culture and the different characteristics that further explain the dynamism of the theory across global economies. Also, the findings of this present research can benefit entrepreneurial educators and trainers toward the design of training programmes and entrepreneurship curriculum that reflect the appropriate skill set required to drive entrepreneurial firms. The reports provided from this study reflect the right entrepreneurial competencies that are required by aspiring, emerging and existing entrepreneurs in the informal sector to achieve higher levels of innovation performance within the changing and highly competitive business environment. As such, the curriculum design and training modules should reflect adequate capacity building for the entrepreneurs. The valuable contributions, however, call for further research attention that can extend the entrepreneurial competencies theory by investigating a cross-country perspective of developing economies to understand the macro-level effects of entrepreneurial competencies on SMEs sustainability.

Disclosure statement

No potential conflict of interest was reported by the authors.

ORCID

Oyedele Martins Ogundana http://orcid.org/0000-0002-0121-7231

References

Abiodun, A. J., & Ibidunni, A. S. (2014). Strategic orientation and performance of agro-based firms in transition economy. *African Journal of Business Management, 8*(13), 495–501.

Acs, Z. J., Szerb, L., & Autio, E. (2015). The global entrepreneurship and development index. In *Global entrepreneurship and development index 2014* (pp. 39–64). SpringerBriefs in Economics. Cham: Springer. doi:10.1007/978-3-319-14932-5_4

Adeeko, A. E. (2017). *External business environment and entrepreneurial performance of Small and Medium Enterprises (SMEs) in Lagos State, Nigeria* (An unpublished masters dissertation). Babcock University, Ilisan, Nigeria.

Adegbuyi, A. A., Oladele, O. P., Iyiola, O. O., Adegbuyi, O. A., Ogunnaike, O. O., Ibidunni, A. S., & Fadeyi, O. I. (2018). Assessing the influence of entrepreneurial orientation on small and medium enterprises' performance. *International Journal of Entrepreneurship, 22*(4), 1–7.

Ahmad, N. H., Ramayah, T., Wilson, C., & Kummerow, L. (2010). Is entrepreneurial competency and business success relationship contingent upon business environment?: A study of Malaysian SMEs. *International Journal of Entrepreneurial Behavior & Research, 16*(3), 182–203.

Akinruwa, T. E., Awolusi, O. D., & Ibojo, B. O. (2013). Determinants of Small & Medium Enterprises (SMEs) Performance in Ekiti State, Nigeria: A business survey approach. *European Journal of Humanities & Social Sciences, 27*(1), 1397–1413.

Akintimehin, O. O., Eniola, A. A., Alabi, O. J., Eluyela, D. F., Okere, W., & Ozordi, E. (2019). Social capital and its effect on business performance in the Nigeria informal sector. *Heliyon, 5*(7), e02024.

Aliyu, M. S. (2017). Entrepreneurial Competencies and the Performance of Small and Medium Enterprises (SMEs) in Zaria Local Government Area of Kaduna State. *International Journal of Entrepreneurial Development, Education and Science Research, 4*(2), 116–218.

Aruni, W., Akira, K., & Hironori, Y. (2014). Entrepreneurial competencies and entrepreneurial orientation of tea manufacturing firms in Sri Lanka. *Asian Social Science, 10*(18), 50–62.

Asalaye, A. J., Popoola, O., Lawal, A. I., Ogundipe, A., & Ezenwoke, O. (2018). The credit channels of monetary policy transmission: Implications on output and employment in Nigeria. *Banks and Bank Systems, 13*(4), 103–118.

Bagozzi, R. P., & Yi, Y. (1988). On the evaluation of structural equation models. *Journal of the Academy of Marketing Science, 16*, 74–94.

Bank of Industry. (2018). *Economic development through the Nigerian Informal Sector: A BOI perspective*. Retrieved from https://www.boi.ng/wp-content/uploads/2018/05/BOI-Working-Paper-Series-No2_Economic-Development-through-the-Nigerian-Informal-Sector-A-BOI-perspective.pdf

Barney, J. (1991). Firm resources and sustained competitive advantage. *Journal of Management, 17*(1), 99–120.

Bartlett, C. A., & Ghoshal, S. (1997). The myth of the general manager: New personal competencies for new management roles. *California Management Review, 40*(1), 92–116.

Bartlett, J. E., Kotrlik, I. J. W., & Higgins, C. C. (2001). Organizational research: Determining the appropriate sample size in survey research. *Information Technology, Learning and Performance Journal, 19*(1), 43–50.

Baum, J. R. (1994). *The relationship of traits, competencies, motivation, strategy and structure to venture growth* (PhD dissertation). University of Maryland, College Park, MD.

Baum, J. R., Locke, E. A., & Smith, K. G. (2001). A multidimensional model of venture growth. *Academy of Management Journal, 44*(2), 292–303.

Bello, S., Robort, G., & Iliyasu, Y. (2015). Effect of entrepreneurial skills management & funding on small & medium enterprises' performances at the Local Government Level in Northern Nigeria. *International Journal of Academic Research in Business & Social Sciences, 5*(6), 338–348.

Berthod, O. (2016). Institutional theory of organizations. In A. Farazmand (Ed.), *Global encyclopedia of public administration, public policy, and governance* (pp. 1–5). Springer International Publishing AG. doi:10.1007/978-3-319-31816-5_63-1

Bird, B. (1995). Toward a theory of entrepreneurial competency. In J. A. Katz & R. H. Brockhaus Sr. (Eds.), *Advances in entrepreneurship, Firm emergence, and growth* (Vol. 2, pp. 51–72). Greenwich, CN: JAI Press.

Bird, B. (2019). Reflection on entrepreneurial competency. In J. Katz & A. Corbet (Eds.), *Seminal ideas for the next twenty-five years of advances: Vol. 21. Advances in entrepreneurship, firm emergence and growth* (pp. 133–140). Emerald Publishing Limited. doi:10.1108/S1074-754020190000021005

Cadbury World. (2014). *History of Cadbury*. Retrieved from www.englishteastore.comandhttps://www.cadbury.co.uk/our-story

Chandler, G., & Jansen, E. (1992). The founder's self-assessed competence and venture performance. *Journal of Business Venturing, 7*, 223–236.

Chandler, G. N., & Hanks, S. H. (1994). Founder competence, the environment and venture performance. *Entrepreneurship: Theory and Practice, 18*(3), 77–90.

Christian, A. (2019). *There is A Village in Nigeria that generates USD 4 Mn every 24 hours – Her's all you need to know*. Retrieved from https://weetracker.com/2019/05/30/computer-village-nigeria-usd-2-bn-revenue/

Cohen, J. (1988). *Statistical power analysis for the behavioral sciences* (2nd ed.). Hillsdale, NJ: Lawrence Erlbaum Associates, Publishers.

Colombo, M. G., & Grilli, L. (2005). Founders' human capital and the growth of new technology-based firms: A competency-based view. *Research Policy, 34*(6), 795–816.

Covin, J.G., and Slevin, D.P. (1989). Strategic management of small firms in hostile and benign environments. *Strategic Management Journal, 10*, 75–87. doi:10.1002/(ISSN)1097-0266

Damilola, O., Deborah, I., Oyedele, O., & Kehinde, A. A. (2020). Global pandemic and business performance. *International Journal of Research in Business and Social Science (2147-4478), 9*(6), 1–11.

Dolz, C., Iborra, M., & Safón, V. (2018). Improving the likelihood of SME survival during financial and economic crises: The importance of TMTs and family ownership for ambidexterity. *Business Research Quarterly, 22*, 119–136.

Endi, G., Surachwon, S., Armanu, K., & Dijumilah, A. (2013). Promoting appropriate technologies for SMEs development through commercialization of research findings. A paper presented during the NASME (National Association of Small & Medium Enterprises). In *International Conference & Exhibition at Abuja Sheraton Hotels & Towers* (Unpublished). Abuja, Nigeria.

Fabrizio, G., Paolo, G., & Alessandra, T. (2011). Entrepreneurial competencies and firm performance: An empirical study (March 31, 2011). In *VIII International Workshop on Human Resource Management - Seville, May 12–13, 2011 - Conference Proceedings*. Retrieved from https://ssrn.com/abstract=1850878

Fabrizio, P., & Alessandra, B. (2011). Entrepreneurship & small industry development in the Commonwealth: An overview. *Nigerian Management Review*, 7(1&2), 443–454.

Fajana, S. (2008). The Nigerian informal economy: Instigating decent work and pay, and national development through unionisation. *Employee Relations*, 30(4), 372–390.

Fapohunda, M. T. (2012). Women and the informal sector in Nigeria: Implications for development. *British Journal of Arts and Social Sciences*, 4(1), 35–45.

Fitzgerald, R. (2005). Products, firms and consumption: Cadbury and the development of marketing, 1900–1939. *Business History*, 47(4), 511–531.

Fornell, C. G., & Larcker, D. F. (1981). Evaluating structural equation models with unobservable variables and measurement error. *Journal of Marketing Research*, 18(1), 39–50.

Gaganis, C., Pasiouras, F., & Voulgari, F. (2019). Culture, business environment and SMEs' profitability: Evidence from European Countries. *Economic Modelling*, 78, 275–292.

Grant, R. M. (1991). The resource-based theory of competitive advantage: Implications for strategy formulation. *California Management Review*, 33, 114–135.

Gümüsay, A. A., & Bohné, T. M. (2018). Individual and organisational inhibitors to the development of entrepreneurial competencies in universities. *Research Policy*, 47, 363–378.

Gwadabe, U. M., & Amirah, N. A. (2017). Entrepreneurial competencies: SMES performance factor in the challenging Nigerian Economy. *Academic Journal of Economic Studies*, 3(4), 55–61.

Hair, J. F., Anderson, R. E., Tatham, R. L., & Black, W. C. (1998). *Multivariate data analysis with readings* (5th ed.). Englewood Cliffs, NJ: Prentice-Hall.

Hair, J. F., Risher, J. J., Sarstedt, M., & Ringle, C. M. (2019). When to use and how to report the results of PLS-SEM. *European Business Review*, 31(1), 2–24.

Hood, J. N., & Young, J. E. (1993). Entrepreneurship's requisite areas of development: A survey of top executives in successful entrepreneurial firms. *Journal of Business Venturing*, 8, 115–135.

Ibidunni, A. S., Kolawole, A. I., Olokundun, M. A., & Ogbari, M. E. (2020). Knowledge transfer and innovation performance of small and medium enterprises: An informal economy analysis. *Heliyon*, 6(8), e04740.

Ibidunni, A. S., Mozie, C., & Ayeni, A. W. (2020). Entrepreneurial characteristics among university students: Insights for understanding entrepreneurial intentions among youths in an emerging economy. *Education+Training*. doi:10.1108/ET-09-2019-0204

Ibidunni, A. S., Ogunnaike, O. O., & Abiodun, A. J. (2017). Extending the knowledge strategy concept: Linking organisational knowledge with strategic orientations. *Academy of Strategic Management Journal*, 16(3), 1–11.

Ibidunni, A. S., Olokundun, M. A., Oke, A. O., & Nwaomonoh, I. C. (2017a). Enhancing the performance of agro-based SMEs: The role of entrepreneurship competencies. *Covenant Journal of Entrepreneurship*, 1(1), 44–51.

Ibidunni, O. S., Iyiola, O., & Ibidunni, A. S. (2014). Product innovation, a survival strategy for small and medium enterprises in Nigeria. *European Scientific Journal*, 10(1), 194–209.

Ibidunni, O. S., & Ogundele, J. K. (2013). Competition in marketing, survival yardstick for small and medium enterprises in Nigeria. *Mediterranean Journal of Social Sciences*, 4(1), 231–240.

Ifekwem, N., & Adedamola, O. (2016). Growth strategies and sustainability of small and medium enterprises in the Oshodi-Isolo Local Government Area of Lagos State. *Acta Univ. Sapientiae, Economics and Business*, 4, 103–118.

Ikadeh, M. S., & Cloete, C. E. (2020). The impact of shopping centre development on informal and small businesses in Lagos, Nigeria. *Journal of Business and Retail Management Research*, 14(3), 1–10.

ILO. (2002). *The informal sector*. Retrieved from https://www.ilo.org/global/about-the-ilo/multimedia/video/video-news-releases/WCMS_074529/lang–en/index.htm

IMF. (2019). *Informality and gender gaps going hand in hand*. Retrieved from https://www.imf.org/~/media/Files/Publications/WP/2019/WPIEA2019112.ashx

Ingenbleek, P. T. (2019). The endogenous African Business: Why and how it is different, Why it is emerging now and why it matters. *Journal of African Business, 20*(2), 195–205.

Jansen, J. J. P., Van Den Bosch, F. A., & Volberda, H. W. (2006). Exploratory innovation, exploitative innovation, and performance: Effects of organisational antecedents and environmental moderators. *Management Science, 52*(11), 1661–1674.

Jevwegaga, H., Ade-adeniji, O., Ibidunni, A. S., Olokundun, M. A., Borishade, T. T., Falola, H. O., ... Ogunniyi, A. (2018). Role of SMEs' entrepreneurial activities and industrial clustering on SMEs' performance. *Academy of Entrepreneurship Journal, 24*(1), 1–7, 1528-2686-24-1-127.

Johnson, S., & Winterton, J. (1999). *Management skills, skills task force research paper 3.* London: Department for Education and Employment.

Kesinro, O. R., Adenugba, A. A., & Ademilua, A. V. (2018). New product development and consumer brand adoption in SMEs manufacturing industry in Ogun State Nigeria. *International Journal of Economics and Management Sciences, 7*(1), 488–509.

Kiggundu, M. N. (2012). Entrepreneurs & entrepreneurship in Africa: What is known & what needs to be done. *Journal of Developmental Entrepreneurship, 7*(3), 239–258.

Lerner, M., & Almor, T. (2002). Relationships among strategic capabilities and the performance of women-owned small ventures. *Journal of Small Business Management, 40*(2), 109–125.

Madichie, N. (2009). Breaking the glass ceiling in Nigeria: A review of women's entrepreneurship. *Journal of African Business, 10*(1), 51–66.

Madichie, N. O., Hinson, R. E., & Ibrahim, M. (2013). A reconceptualisation of entrepreneurial orientation in an emerging market insurance company. *Journal of African Business, 14*(3), 202–214.

Madichie, N. O., Mpofu, K., & Kolo, J. (2017). Entrepreneurship development in Africa: Insights from Nigeria's and Zimbabwe's telecoms. In A. Akinyoade, N. O. Madichie et al. 239 T. Dietz, & C. U. Uche (Eds.), *Entrepreneurship in Africa* (Vol. 15, pp. 172–208). Leiden, The Netherlands: Brill Publishing.

Man, T. W. Y. (2001). *Entrepreneurial competencies and the performance of small and medium enterprises in the Hong Kong Services Sector* (Unpublished Thesis).

Man, T. W. Y., Lau, T., & Chan, K. F. (2002). The competitiveness of small and medium enterprises: A conceptualisation with focus on entrepreneurial competencies. *Journal of Business Venturing, 17*(2), 123–142.

Man, T. W. Y., Lau, T., & Snape, E. (2008). Entrepreneurial competencies and the performance of small and medium enterprises: An investigation through a framework of competitiveness. *Journal of Small Business and Entrepreneurship, 23*(3), 257–276.

Miles, M. P., Covin, J. G., & Heeley, M. B. (2000, Spring). The relationship between environmental dynamism and small firm structure, strategy, and performance. *Journal of Marketing Theory and Practice, 8*, 63–75.

Mitchell, R. K., Busenitz, L., Lant, T., McDougall, P., Morse, E. A., & Smith, B. (2002). Toward a theory of entrepreneurial cognition: Rethinking the people side of entrepreneurship research. *Entrepreneurship Theory and Practice, 27*, 93–104.

Mitchelmore, S., & Rowley, J. (2010). Entrepreneurial competencies: A literature review and development agenda. *International Journal of Entrepreneurial Behaviour & Research, 16*(2), 92–111.

National Social Investments Programme. (2020, September 15). *N-Power programme.* Retrieved from https://n-sip.gov.ng/npower/

Nerisa, P. D. B. A. (2015). Business University Student Entrepreneurial Competencies: Towards Readiness for Globalization. *Advances in Economics and Business, 3*(9), 390–397.

Obaji, N. O., & Olugu, M. U. (2014). The role of government policy in entrepreneurship development. *Science Journal of Business and Management, 2*(4), 109–115.

Obiwuru, T. C., Oluwalaiye, O. B., & Okwu, A. T. (2011). External and internal environment of businesses in Nigeria: An appraisal. *International Bulletin of Business Administration, 12*, 15–23.

OECD. (2018, February 22–23). *Developing entrepreneurship competencies: Policy note.* 2018 SME Ministerial Conference, Mexico City.

Ogundana, O. (2020a). *Factors influencing the business growth of women-owned sewing businesses (WOSBs) in Lagos-State, Nigeria: A gender-aware growth framework* (Doctoral dissertation). Nottingham Trent University. Retrieved from https://bit.ly/2S5QKMp

Ogundana, O. (2020b). Obstacles facing women-owned enterprises: A case for Sub-Sahara African women. *World Review of Entrepreneurship, Management and Sustainable Development*.

Ogundana, O., Galanakis, K., Simba, A., & Oxborrow, L. (2018a). Women-owned sewing businesses in Lagos-State, Nigeria: A study of the factors influencing their business growth. In *BAM 2018 Conference proceedings*. London: British Academy of Management. Retrieved from https://irep.ntu.ac.uk/id/eprint/38368/1/1237540_Ogundana.pdf

Ogundana, O., Galanakis, K., Simba, A., & Oxborrow, L. (2018b). Factors influencing the business growth of women-owned sewing businesses in Lagos-State, Nigeria: A pilot study. *Organisational Studies and Innovation Review, 4*(2), 25–36.

Ogundana, O., Galanakis, K., Simba, A., & Oxborrow, L. (2019). Growth perception amongst women entrepreneurs: An emerging economy perspective. *International Journal of Entrepreneurship and Small Business*.

Rasmussen, E., Mosey, S., & Wright, M. (2011). The evolution of entrepreneurial competencies: A longitudinal study of university spin-off venture. *Journal of Management Studies, 48*(6), 1314–1345.

Saidu, S., & Dauda, U. (2014). Tax evasion and governance challenges in the Nigerian Informal Sector. *Journal of Finance and Economics, 2*(5), 56–161. Retrieved from http://pubs.sciepub.com/jfe/2/5/4/

Shehnaz, T., & Ramayah, T. (2015). Entrepreneurial competencies & SMEs business success: The contingent role of external integration. *Mediterranean Journal of Social Sciences MCSER Publishing, 6*(1), 50–61.

Shepherd, D. A. (1999). Venture capitalists' assessment of new venture survival. *Management Science, 45*, 621–632.

SMEDAN. (2017). *National Survey of Micro Small & Medium Enterprises (MSMEs) 2017*. Retrieved from https://www.msmehub.org/article/2019/07/nbs-smedan-national-survey-on-micro-small-and-medium-enterprises-msmes-2017.

Solesvik, M. Z. (2012). Entrepreneurial competencies in emerging context. In *17th Nordic Conference on Small Business Research* (pp. 9–23). Helsinki.

Stuart, R., & Lindsay, P. (1997). Beyond the frame of management competencies: Towards a contextually embedded framework of managerial competence in organisations. *Journal of European Industrial Training, 21*(1), 26–34.

Thomas, I., & Herrisier, R. L. (1991). *Managerial competencies for effective performance at senior levels in government*. Hong Kong: Senior Staff Course.

Uzairu, M. G., & Noor, A. A. (2017). Entrepreneurial competencies: SMEs performance factor in the challenging Nigerian Economy. *Academic Journal of Economic Studies, 3*(4), 55–61.

Weerakoon, C., & Kodithuwakku, S. S. (2018). Entrepreneurial competencies and entrepreneurial orientation: Moderating effects of firm age and firm size. *Journal of Asia Entrepreneurship and Sustainability, 14*(1), 75–100.

Welter, F. (2011). Contextualising entrepreneurship - Challenges and ways forward. *Entrepreneurship Theory and Practice, 35*(1), 165–184.

White, S. (2004). *Donor approaches to improving the business environment for small enterprises— Working group on enabling environment, a committee of donor agencies for small enterprise development*, Washington.

Wijbenga, F., & Van Witteloostuijn, A. (2007). Entrepreneurial locus of control and competitive strategies: The moderating effect of environmental dynamism. *Journal of Economic Psychology, 28*, 566–589.

Zizile, T., & Tendai, C. (2018). The importance of entrepreneurial competencies on the performance of women entrepreneurs in South Africa. *Journal of Applied Business Research (JABR), 34*(2), 223–236.

Against the Norm? Entrepreneurial Human Capital, Gender and Resource Mobilization in Sub-saharan Africa

Ikenna Uzuegbunam, Rachida Aïssaoui and Amy Taylor-Bianco

ABSTRACT

This study examines how entrepreneurial human capital affects the resource mobilization process in new ventures, specifically the likelihood of using informal ties (i.e. family and friends) in their hiring process. Building on human capital arguments, we theorize that the higher the entrepreneur's formal educational attainment, the greater the likelihood that they will go against the norm of hiring through informal ties. Given the centrality of gender in the relationship between entrepreneurship and family embeddedness, we evaluate the moderating role of gender on the relationship between formal education and the hiring process. Empirical findings from logistic regression analyses of 1,114 new ventures in Nigeria provide broad support for the theoretical framework. These findings contribute to our understanding of individual-level forces that influence the persistence of, or decreased reliance on, informal institutions in entrepreneurial activity in Sub-Saharan Africa.

1. Introduction

A central concern of the entrepreneurship literature is how entrepreneurs mobilize resources that will enable them to exploit a market opportunity. A recent review of the prior literature supports the notion that the principal resources that are most often mobilized in new ventures are human capital, social capital, and financial capital (Clough, Fang, Vissa, & Wu, 2019). Yet, an overwhelming majority of prior work in this research stream has focused on how entrepreneurs acquire financial capital (e.g. Hallen, 2008; Hsu, 2007; Khayesi & George, 2011; Khayesi, George, & Antonakis, 2014), with limited research attention to how entrepreneurs assemble human capital for their new ventures.

The institutional view in entrepreneurship, which focuses on the role of institutions in entrepreneurial activities, provides an opportunity to reexamine resource mobilization by nascent firms. Specifically, institutional theorists have shed important light on the ways formal and informal institutions – respectively defined as the explicit and implicit rules guiding organizational and social behaviors (North, 1990) – uniquely affect entrepreneurs' access to valuable resources. Despite these insights in the prior literature, the lack of research that looks at interactions between institutional components is a serious limitation in this research agenda (Cuervo-Cazurra, Gaur, & Singh, 2019).

This study leverages the Nigerian entrepreneurial landscape to address this shortcoming in the institutional entrepreneurship literature. Nigerian firms have traditionally relied on informal institutions to access human capital, as manifested in the practice known as the *man-know-man* syndrome (Ituma & Simpson, 2009). *Man-know-man*, which reflects Nigeria's relationship orientation (Hofstede & Hofstede, 2005) has long substituted for the weakness of formal institutions in supporting entrepreneurial activities in Nigeria (Hack-Polay, Igwe, & Madichie, 2020; Nafziger, 1969). The institutional practice of hiring through informal ties is not specific to Nigeria. Rather, this practice has been observed in many emerging economies characterized by weak formal institutions (Acquaah, 2012; Ahlstrom & Bruton, 2006).

Notwithstanding the potential advantages that entrepreneurs can gain from drawing on family and friends for new venture resources, there is evidence to suggest that this sort of practice can also be very costly (Nafziger, 1969). For instance, using a sample of Ugandan entrepreneurs, Khayesi et al. (2014) demonstrate that the cost of raising financial resources from kin outweighs the benefit from raising such resources. Similarly, Amankwah-Amoah, Ifere, and Nyuur (2016) show through Nigerian and Ghanaian data that the tendency to rely on family and friends for human capital is often detrimental to firms because it can prevent hiring of higher quality employees, or firing of underperforming employees.

Importantly, globalization forces have fostered the broad adoption of pro-reforms by emerging countries (Cuervo-Cazurra et al., 2019), which are supported both by a strengthening of formal institutions (Peng, Sun, Pinkham, & Chen, 2009), and by the modernization of industrial sectors reflected, among others, in preference for democracy, higher educational levels, openness to change, respect for individual freedom, changes in gender roles, and a gradual move away from traditional practices (Fukuyama, 2009; Inglehart, 1991). Nigeria's rise to a democratic system in 1999 has indeed been accompanied by economic reforms (Ezema & Ogujiuba, 2012) and improvements in its formal educational levels (World Bank, 2020a). It remains unclear how such modernizing forces in a country's institutional environment will impact traditional resource mobilization practice of hiring through informal ties.

Therefore, the purpose of this study is to examine how individual-level factors affect entrepreneurs' tendency to resort to informal institutions for access to human capital. Specifically, we focus on entrepreneurial human capital, namely their formal educational attainment, which is likely to alter an entrepreneur's calculus toward informal ties. As such, the expectation is that entrepreneurs with higher levels of formal education are less likely to perpetuate traditional hiring practices such as *man-know-man*. Furthermore, given the centrality of gender roles in traditional societies, and in the relationship between entrepreneurship and family (e.g. Henry, Foss, & Ahl, 2016; Igwe, Odunukan, et al., 2020; Jennings & Brush, 2013), we also test this argument against gender differences.

Empirically, we analyze survey data from a sample of 1,114 new ventures in Nigeria. We examine whether increases in the entrepreneur's formal education will affect the likelihood of employing traditional hiring norms such as the *man-know-man* practice. We focus on the Nigerian economy as it provides a novel and strong context to test our arguments regarding the role of education and gender in either perpetuating or hindering this informal institution. The next section summarizes the relevant institutional view in the entrepreneurship literature and outlines the theoretical arguments of this paper. The theory section is followed by a description of the empirical context, data, and analysis. Then, key findings are presented and discussed. Finally, we conclude with a discussion of implications and limitations.

2. Theory and hypotheses

Institutional scholars in entrepreneurship generally acknowledge the significance of informal institutions in the strategy and performance of entrepreneurs, especially in the context of developing economies (Hack-Polay et al., 2020; Igwe, Odunukan, et al., 2020; Igwe, Madichie, & Amoncar, 2020). A stream of the literature shows that the pull of informal institutions is likely to diminish in importance as formal institutions become stronger (Chang, 2011; Liu, Keller, & Hong, 2014; Peng, Wang, & Jiang, 2008). For instance, Luo, Huang, and Wang (2012) find that as formal institutions in China became stronger, organizations increased their use of market mechanisms. Similarly, Horak (2017) noted that the Korean cultural practices have experienced major changes following the Asian financial crisis of 1997–1998 and the pressure to internationalize Korean firms. Fajana, Owoyemi, Elegbede, and Gbajumo-Sheriff (2011) found that Nigeria's rise to a democratic system in 1999 has enhanced the use of Western human resource practices in Nigerian organizations. In sum, internationalization and deregulation of markets, changes in a country's political or economic systems, and globalization in general (Ahlstrom & Bruton, 2006; Fajana et al., 2011; Jackson, 2004) have thus been identified as major factors affecting changes in existing informal institutions. We draw on these arguments to consider a significant but often overlooked aspect of resource mobilization strategies in new ventures, specifically examining how the development of human capital might impact entrepreneurs' hiring practices in Sub-Saharan Africa.

2.1. Founders education and the tendency toward informal ties

The entrepreneur's educational background is widely researched in terms of its human capital function, direct or indirect, on new venture processes and outcomes (Ding, 2011; Gimeno, Folta, Cooper, & Woo, 1997; Hallen, 2008; Hsu, 2007). The general notion is that increased education enables the acquisition of general human capital (Cooper, Gimeno-Gascon, & Woo, 1994), which positively influences access to resources (Hallen, 2008), and entrepreneurial performance (Brüderl, Preisendorfer, & Ziegler, 1992). Due to its broad applicability in different contexts, formal education increases the opportunity set for entrepreneurs and presents a higher order of opportunity costs for the entrepreneur since they might be able to deploy their effort in an alternative setting. Thus, formal education is expected to increase the threshold of performance in the entrepreneur's chosen activity (Gimeno et al., 1997), which implies that educated entrepreneurs have an incentive to pursue strategies that will maximize the performance of their ventures.

Interestingly, little is known about the effects of education on perpetuating traditional norms such as the *man-know-man*, and more specifically on the entrepreneur's ability and/or willingness to resort to family members for support (Kotha & George, 2012). Arregle et al. (2013, p. 24) called for research on "how different levels of education and prior experience (and other demographic attributes) influence the ways entrepreneurs use and manage family ties."

Historically, emerging market countries have low levels of wealth and education. Nigeria, for instance, is considered a poor country in terms of GDP per capita, ranking 133 of 183 countries in 2019 (World Bank, 2020b). Similarly, in 2018, Nigeria ranked 158 out of 189 countries on the Education Index developed by the United Nations Development Program.[1] It is therefore not surprising that traditional practices such as *man-know-man* are commonplace in emerging countries, notably as they reflect a broad tendency to rely on the extended family to access scarce or difficult-to-access resources. There are also reciprocal obligations embedded in *man-know-man* societies as entrepreneurs often feel the need to assist extended family members as they gain more prosperity. Such assistance can entail entrepreneurs offering family and friends opportunities for employment or apprenticeships in their businesses. For instance, Igwe, Madichie et al. (2020) capture these complicated networks of family embeddedness in their study of the Igbo businesses in South Eastern Nigeria. Further, Nafziger's (1969) account illustrates this point: *"Over a period of years, the extended family of the entrepreneur has incurred a number of (social) claims and obligations, which can be satisfied in part when selecting a labor force. In some instances, the entrepreneur may be pressed to hire a laborer or train an apprentice from some family to whom his family is obligated. On the other hand, it may be difficult for the entrepreneur to find persons to evaluate applicants outside of his home village"* (p. 30).

Given this tendency toward informal ties, how does formal education limit family embeddedness in new ventures? As individuals become more educated in a formal setting, their social networks will broaden. This will greatly enhance their ability to find employees outside of their immediate network of family and friends. Furthermore, as they gain more education, their threshold for higher performance will increase, making them less likely to abide by such practices. More educated entrepreneurs tend to incorporate business choices that engender higher economic performance by broadening their opportunity set (Carraher, Welsh, & Svilokos, 2016; Gimeno et al., 1997; Welsh, Kaciak, & Shamah, 2018). In fact, recent evidence suggests that a critical way of distinguishing between opportunity and necessity entrepreneurs is that opportunity entrepreneurs tend to hire non-familial individuals as a means of growing their businesses, whereas necessity entrepreneurs do not (Dimova & Pela, 2018). Thus, for more educated individuals, the decision to pursue a more differentiated entrepreneurial opportunity will be subsequently accompanied by an emphasis on formalizing new venture strategies that would increase the odds of success of the venture (e.g. formalizing hiring practices). As such, we hypothesize that:

Hypothesis 1. Founders with more formal education will be more likely to deviate from norms of hiring employees through informal ties (i.e. *man-know-man*).

---

[1] Please see http://hdr.undp.org/en/data#, Accessed December 4, 2020.

2.2. The moderating effects of family situation

A central tenet of the preceding arguments is that formal education weakens the entrepreneur's social bond with family and friends by turning them toward more formal channels (e.g. advertisements) for seeking employees. Yet, we need to account for the role of the entrepreneur's family situation in this important decision regarding how to hire employees for the new venture. In particular, the presence of young children in an entrepreneur's life has been shown to impact entrepreneurial choices, including the decision of whether to start a new venture (Aldrich & Cliff, 2003; Jennings & Brush, 2013), or exit from an existing venture (Justo, Detienne, & Sieger, 2015).

We anticipate that the presence of young children will reduce the likelihood that entrepreneurs will deviate from hiring employees through informal ties. First, though formal education increases the opportunity cost of underperformance (Gimeno et al., 1997), entrepreneurs with young children might have a lowered threshold of entrepreneurial performance due to their parental and childcare obligations. Thus, the presence of young children might reconfigure an educated entrepreneur's predisposition for opportunity entrepreneurship toward necessity entrepreneurship, by reducing the amount of time the entrepreneur can spend on their business (Williams, 2004).

Second, the presence of young children might act as a bonding mechanism between the entrepreneurs and their family and friends. Parents of young children are often more likely to seek or be enveloped by family and friends because they would prioritize social support for their children through these informal networks (e.g. childcare or playmates). In doing so, they are inadvertently drawn toward the traditional societal norm of reciprocal obligations between them and their informal ties of family and friends. We expect that this normative force of relying on family and friends, which also has instrumental value for parents of young children will outweigh the effect of formal education on their hiring strategy. We therefore propose that:

Hypothesis 2. Family situation moderates the relationship between formal education and hiring through informal ties such that the divergent effect of formal education on hiring through informal ties will be lower for entrepreneurs with young children.

2.3. Gender differences in the moderating role of family situation

As indicated in the preceding analysis, the founder's family situation is key to understanding entrepreneurial processes and outcomes (Arraiz, 2018). But the above arguments are implicitly genderless. However, recent research provides ample theory and evidence of a gendered view of entrepreneurship, especially as it applies to the impact of the family situation on gender differences (e.g. Henry et al., 2016: Jennings & Brush, 2013; Madichie, 2009). This research points to prominent differences between male and female entrepreneurs (e.g. Aldrich & Cliff, 2003; Coleman & Robb, 2009; Cruz, Justo, & De Castro, 2012; Fairlie & Robb, 2009; Jennings & McDougald, 2007; Justo et al., 2015; Kanze, Huang, Conley, & Higgins, 2018). Differences that are reified in less developed societies where gender roles are highly segregated (Amine & Staub, 2009; Aragon-Mendoza, Pardo Del Val, & Roig-Dobon, 2016; Ituma & Simpson, 2009; Woldie &

Adersua, 2004), such as emerging market countries generally characterized by traditional gender roles where women are expected to be the nurturers and caretakers of family concerns (Becker, 1985; Cruz et al., 2012; Welsh et al., 2018) whether themselves or through coordination of other caregiver and household responsibilities (Casper, Harris, Taylor-Bianco, & Wayne, 2011). Female entrepreneurs, more than their male counterparts, are expected to comply with their social obligations and this competing force often compels women to prioritize the needs of their family members (Jennings & McDougald, 2007) above and beyond work obligations. This stereotypical view of women imposes a significant barrier that prevents them from investing in more market-based activities (Becker, 1985).

Given these social expectations, female entrepreneurs are less likely to segment their family situation from their work-life than men (Jennings & McDougald, 2007). Brush (1992) found that for women, the venture creation process is more integrated with family role responsibilities than segmented from them (see also Cruz et al., 2012; Fairlie & Robb, 2009). Furthermore, Coleman and Robb (2009) demonstrate that women entrepreneurs also tend to rely on informal sources for entrepreneurial resources, which could be either as a result of their need to balance family and work responsibilities (Madichie, 2009) or due to discrimination they face in financial markets and the broader institutional environment (Ncube, Soonawalla, & Hausken, 2019). For instance, Woldie and Adersua (2004) and Madichie (2009, 2011) suggest that female entrepreneurs in Nigeria frequently confront the opportunity cost of furthering their career versus building their families. They often have to choose between their family/motherhood and their business. Madichie (2011, p. 216) further made the interesting point that "women and success might have to be a zero-sum game where successful businesswomen would have to be failures in other departments."[2] Justo et al. (2015) extended this line of reasoning by considering the effects of being a father or mother on entrepreneurial activity and while they found that overall male entrepreneurs were less influenced by their family situation than women, being the parent of young children who need more parental care (in particular) versus being the parent of young adults who are presumably more self-sufficient also yielded additional gender differences (see also Davis & Shaver, 2012). In particular, having young children constitute a deeper hurdle for women entrepreneurs (Justo et al., 2015) than for men. As eloquently summarized by an experienced female entrepreneur "being a woman per se is probably not as big an issue as being a wife and mother" (Moult & Anderson, 2005, p. 264). Therefore, we expect between gender differences where the negative moderating effect of the family situation on formal education's relationship with hiring through informal ties will be more severe for female entrepreneurs compared to their male counterparts.

Hypothesis 3. There is a gender difference in the moderating impact of family situation on the relationship between formal education and hiring through informal ties such that there is less divergence from the norms for female founders than for male founders.

---

[2] Indeed, Becker (1985) in his study of western economies notes this complex tradeoff, stating "Childcare and other housework are tiring and limit access to jobs requiring travel or odd hours" (p. S35). The entrepreneurial occupation fits this profile where the individual will be tasked to work extremely long hours, often traveling as they network to acquire resources for their new venture.

3. Research method and analysis

3.1. Empirical context and sample

Nigeria is the most populated country in Africa, situated in the Sub-Saharan westbound of the continent. Nigeria boasts the largest population in Africa, with about 182 million residents (Amankwah-Amoah et al., 2016; United Nations, 2017a; World Bank, 2015), and one of the fastest growing populations with predictions that its population will surpass that of the United States by 2050 (United Nations, 2017b). Despite an abundant supply of natural and human resources, and a very diverse economy, Nigeria is struggling to rise above its lower middle-income status, and faces high levels of unemployment (Dimova & Pela, 2018; Owualah, 1999; World Bank, 2017). As such, the Nigerian government has initiated policies, and programs aimed at embracing a capital market economy (Hoskisson, Eden, Lau, & Wright, 2000), and fostering entrepreneurial activities (Ihugba, Odii, & Njoku, 2013; Inyang & Enuoh, 2009; Owualah, 1999). These initiatives, though, have not yet proven successful in addressing some of the challenges facing entrepreneurship in Nigeria (Ihugba et al., 2013), as well as corruption and nepotism (Azolukwan & Perkins, 2009). These challenges are further exacerbated for the female Nigerian entrepreneur due to cultural expectations related to segregated gender roles (Madichie, 2011). Thus, Nigeria provides an interesting field to examine our research question, that is, how a human capital construct such as formal education can influence whether an entrepreneur will rely on informal institutions.

The data for this research are drawn from the 2007 World Bank Enterprise Survey on Nigerian establishments (see Enterprise Surveys [http://www.enterprisesurveys.org]; e.g. Bardasi, Sabarwal, & Terrell, 2011). This World Bank survey was administered using a face-to-face interview format to 2,387 establishments in 11 states of Nigeria between September 2007 and February 2008. The primary respondents to the survey are the manager/owner/director of each establishment. In some instances, these primary respondents were supported by their company accountants and human resource managers.[3] Consistent with our framing, this survey captures the post-1999 time period which represents the most stable democratic period in Nigeria (see Ezema & Ogujiuba, 2012).

We used the following criteria to further delineate our sample for the study. First, we included establishments that are 8 years or younger, consistent with an established practice in prior new venture studies (Arregle et al., 2013). We expect founders of nascent ventures, of this age group, to rely more on informal networks including family and friends. It is, therefore, interesting to observe that some ventures within this age group (in our sample) are deviating from the norms of relying on their informal networks for hiring employees at this early stage of their venture.

Second, we included establishments where the founder is not only the sole or majority owner of the new venture but is also actively involved in managing the venture as the top manager (see Arregle et al., 2013). This criterion allowed us to ensure credible claims about family ties and gender differences, since the founders in our sample are directly involved in decision-making processes in their ventures. Our final sample consists of 1,114 independently founded ventures. This excludes inherited establishments or establishments that are part of a larger firm. The industries represented in the sample include

---

[3]https://microdata.worldbank.org/index.php/catalog/631.

manufacturing, retail, information technology, construction & transport, and hotels & restaurants.

3.2. Variables and measures

3.2.1. Dependent variable

Informal ties, our dependent variable, assesses the degree to which entrepreneurs draw on family and friends for hiring into their new ventures. In the Nigerian context, *family* and *friends'* ties have similar effects as informal components of job referral systems – also known as the *man-know-man* syndrome (Ituma & Simpson, 2009). Consistent with the cultural connotations of extended families in developing countries, we purposefully, conceptualized family to include family members and close friends. We coded this measure from the following survey question, i.e., "How did this establishment finds its most recent employee?" If the respondent answered: "through family/friends" (i.e. informal recruitment ties, also *informal ties*), we coded this as 1, otherwise 0. Fifty-five percent of our sample found their most recent employee through *informal ties*. The other 45% found their employees through one of the following options: "public placement office," "private placement office," "public announcement/advertisement," "school-related network," or "other".

3.2.2. Independent variable

Educational attainment of the primary founder of the business (i.e. either the sole owner, or the majority owner of the venture, who is involved in managing the venture) is the independent variable. Our primary measure of a founder's formal education is the percentage of people in the sample that have attained lower levels of education than a focal founder. The range of this measure is between 0 and 1. It is calculated from 11 categories of the founder's highest level of education (see Table 1 for details of these educational categories). Empirically, this sort of measure is advantageous because it captures both the context of founders' education as well as the empirical distribution of level of education in a given labor supply (Gimeno et al., 1997). In supplemental analyses, we use dummy variables to capture the different categories of educational attainment (Coleman & Robb, 2009; Fairlie & Robb, 2009).

3.2.3. Moderating variables

The first moderating variable captures the *family situation* of the entrepreneur (i.e. the primary/sole owner and top manager of this new venture). Specifically, a dummy variable is coded to capture whether the entrepreneur has children under the age of 10 years. The second moderating variable is the *gender* of the entrepreneur (female founder = 1, male founder = 0).

3.2.4. Control variables

Guided by prior entrepreneurship research (Arregle et al., 2013; Justo et al., 2015), we used control variables related to the individual entrepreneur and their family, industry, and social context. First, we controlled for other relevant entrepreneur's characteristics (i.e. industry experience and age; Welsh et al., 2018). The entrepreneur's industry-specific

TABLE 1 Variables and Definitions.

Variable	Definition
Informal ties	Dummy = 1 if venture found its most recent employee through family/friends, 0 otherwise
Formal education	This measure is based on the founder's highest level of education, where No education = 1, primary school completed = 2, started but did not complete secondary school = 3, secondary school completed = 4, vocational training completed = 5, some university training = 6, undergraduate degree completed (BA, BSc etc.) = 7, MBA from Nigerian university completed = 8, Other post graduate degree (Ph.D., Masters) from Nigerian university completed = 10. From these levels, we calculated the **percentage of people in the sample** that attained lower levels of education than a focal founder (i.e. percentile, in terms of education, Gimeno et al., 1997).
Gender	Dummy = 1 if the founder is female, 0 if male
Young children	Dummy = 1 if founder has children younger than 10 years old
Founder' age	Founder's age bracket. That is, 30 years or less = 1, 31–45 = 2, 46–55 = 3, and ≥ 55 = 4.
Industry experience[†]	Natural logarithm of founder's number of years of managerial experience in the same industry
Industry classification	Industry dummies for trade/service and high technology, where the excluded category is manufacturing and other industries. Trade/service includes the following: retail, construction & transport, and hotels & restaurants. See similar classification in Bureau of Labor and Statistics (BLS) classification of based on occupational and skill similarities (https://www.bls.gov/soc/)
State classification	State dummies for the different Nigerian regions. Nigeria is made up of 36 States and Abuja (Federal Capital Territory, FCT). The survey included ventures from 10 of these states and the FCT (i.e. Abia, Abuja, Anambra, Bauchi, Cross River, Enugu, Kaduna, Kano, Lagos, Ogun, and Sokoto). Lagos is the base (excluded) category.
Sole proprietorship	Dummy = 1, if the new venture is a sole proprietorship.
Firm size[†]	Natural logarithm of establishment's total sales in Naira currency*.
Firm age[†]	Natural logarithm of establishment's age*

See http://www.enterprisesurveys.org for full questionnaire and data access. [†]Variables are in natural logarithms.

experience is a proxy for human capital, and directly affects the entrepreneur's legitimacy in their organizational environment. Similarly, we include a control for the founder's age.

We controlled for firm legal structure (i.e. sole proprietorship as opposed to a partnership, or privately held, limited company) and industry effects. Following Arregle et al.'s (2013) recommendations, we used the following industry categories: high technology; trade/service; and other industries, which includes manufacturing as the referent group. The broad category of trade/service includes the following industries: retail, construction and transport, and hotels and restaurants. Finally, we controlled for the states represented in our sample to capture the unobserved variation in cultural and ethnic tendencies across the country. Table 1 summarizes our measures and their definitions in this study.

3.3. Data analysis method

We use logistic regression as our primary method of analysis because the dependent variable is binary. To mitigate the risk of multicollinearity in our study, we mean-centered the independent variable before entering the interaction terms in our regressions. We note that all our empirical tests are conservative, using two-tailed tests. All variance inflation factors (VIFs) were below 4, well below the acceptable limits of 10.

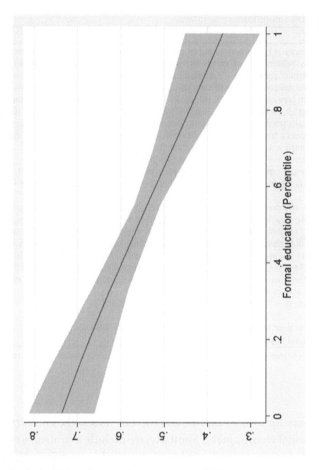

FIGURE 1 Predicted Effect of Education on Man-know-man Hiring.

TABLE 2 Difference in Means Tests Relative to the Dependent Variable.

Independent Variables ↓	Man-know-man (Yes = 1): Mean Difference	T-statistic
Founders with secondary education	0.2238	7.7107 (p= 0.0000)
Founders with vocational education	0.2337	7.8134 (p= 0.0000)
Founders with bachelor's degree	0.3143	3.7523 (p= 0.0002)
Founders with graduate degree	0.2226	1.3381 (p= 0.1811)
Female founders	−0.0702	−2.0232 (p= 0.0433)
Founders with young children	0.0566	1.8823 (p= 0.0601)

Each of the measures in these difference of means tests is a dummy 1, if the condition is fulfilled. Ho (diff) = Mean (control group) − Mean (treatment group) = 0, Ha: diff! = 0 (i.e. either Ha: diff<0 or Ha: diff>0). *P-values* using two-tailed tests are in parentheses next to the T-statistic magnitude.

4. Results

4.1. Hypothesis testing

Table 2 provides the difference of mean tests for the key variables in this study. The results show that there are significant differences in the hiring tendencies of founders that

TABLE 3 Summary Statistics and Correlation Matrix.

	1	2	3	4	5	6	7	8	9	10	11	12	13	14	15
1. Informal hiring ties															
2. Formal education	−0.26														
3. Secondary school	−0.22	0.89													
4. Vocational school	−0.23	0.86	0.75												
5. Bachelor's degree	−0.11	0.31	0.18	0.23											
6. Graduate degree	−0.04	0.16	0.09	0.12	0.49										
7. Formal education × Gender	−0.10	0.47	0.42	0.40	0.16	0.11									
8. Formal education × Young children	−0.18	0.78	0.67	0.65	0.27	0.11	0.37								
9. Founder's gender (Female = 1)	0.06	0.03	0.08	0.01	0.00	0.02	0.05	0.02							
10. Founder's young children (Yes = 1)	−0.06	0.04	0.05	0.02	0.04	0.00	0.02	0.02	−0.01						
11. Founder's industry experience[†]	−0.20	0.04	0.05	0.03	0.07	0.04	0.06	0.00	−0.08	0.12					
12. Founder's age	−0.25	0.18	0.15	0.14	0.17	0.12	0.05	0.12	−0.08	0.18	0.20				
13. Firm size[†]	−0.29	0.28	0.24	0.23	0.17	0.00	0.11	0.20	−0.07	0.03	0.17	0.37			
14. Firm age[†]	−0.17	−0.01	0.02	−0.02	0.04	0.01	0.02	−0.04	−0.08	0.14	0.69	0.15	0.10		
15. Sole proprietorship	0.00	0.05	0.05	0.06	−0.03	−0.01	0.04	0.02	−0.03	0.03	−0.03	−0.05	−0.03	−0.08	
Mean	0.55	0.5	0.52	0.38	0.03	0.01	0	0.01	0.24	0.58	1.67	1.97	15.2	1.53	0.02
S.D.	0.5	0.28	0.5	0.48	0.18	0.09	0.13	0.22	0.43	0.49	0.52	0.8	1.49	0.47	0.15
Min	0	0.01	0	0	0	0	0	0	0	0	0	1	11.4	0	0
Max	1	1	1	1	1	1	−0.49	−0.49	1	1	3.47	4	20.6	2.08	1

Bivariate correlations greater than or equal to absolute value of 0.06, 0.07 and 0.09 are significant at the $p < 0.1$, $p < 0.05$, and $p < 0.01$ respectively. Two-tailed tests. [†] Represents variables that are in natural logarithms.

TABLE 4 Logistic Regressions Predicting Informal Hiring Ties (*Man-know-man*) in New Ventures.

	Model 1	Model 2	Model 3	Model 4	Model 5
	\multicolumn{5}{c}{DV: Dummy = 1, if venture hired through *Informal ties*}
		Full Sample		Female_founded	Male_founded
Formal education		−1.464***	−1.812***	−3.194***	−1.321***
		−0.283	**−0.349**	**−0.581**	**−0.254**
		[0.263]	[0.408]	[0.951]	[0.464]
Formal education × Founder's young children			0.561	2.981**	−0.205
			0.543		
			[0.518]	[1.184]	[0.597]
Founder's young children (Y = 1)	−0.181	−0.157	−0.163	−0.539*	−0.095
				−0.098	
	[0.144]	[0.145]	[0.147]	[0.323]	[0.169]
Founder's gender (Female = 1)	0.197	0.263	0.263		
	[0.161]	[0.162]	[0.162]		
Founder's industry experience†	−0.456**	−0.477**	−0.471**	−0.963**	−0.362
	[0.195]	[0.194]	[0.194]	[0.437]	[0.223]
Founder's age	−0.380***	−0.336***	−0.335***	−0.203	−0.378***
	[0.096]	[0.098]	[0.098]	[0.226]	[0.114]
Firm size†	−0.363***	−0.311***	−0.309***	−0.271**	−0.329***
	[0.053]	[0.055]	[0.055]	[0.122]	[0.063]
Firm age†	−0.283	−0.282	−0.280	−0.074	−0.351
	[0.221]	[0.221]	[0.222]	[0.502]	[0.261]
Sole proprietorship	0.031	0.142	0.161	1.523	0.007
	[0.432]	[0.431]	[0.433]	[1.043]	[0.492]
Constant	7.633***	7.425***	7.563***	7.549***	7.862***
	[0.889]	[0.908]	[0.917]	[1.993]	[1.053]
Industry effects	Yes	Yes	Yes	Yes	Yes
State effects	Yes	Yes	Yes	Yes	Yes
Observations (df_m)	1,114 (21)	1,114 (22)	1,114 (23)	261 (20)	844 (22)
Loglikelihood	−648.6	−632.8	−632.2	−140.8	−477.2
Pseudo R-squared	0.153	0.173	0.174	0.201	0.181
Chi-squared	184.0***	199.0***	200.3***	52.56***	156.0***

*** p < 0.01, ** p < 0.05, * p < 0.1. All tests are two-tailed. Marginal effects for key variables are in parentheses and in bold font. Robust standard errors are in square brackets below coefficients and marginal effects. For ease of presentation, coefficients of industry and state dummies are included in the models but are not shown in the table. † Represents variables that are in natural logarithms.

have attained secondary school education compared to founders without secondary school education ($p < 0.01$). Specifically, founders without secondary school education (control group) have a statistically significant higher tendency toward hiring through informal ties when compared to founders with secondary school education (treatment group). These results are broadly consistent across different levels of education reported in Table 2 (i.e. vocational education and bachelor's degree). Though there is the expected difference in the means for graduate degree holders and the control group, this difference is not statistically significant. Also, we note that Table 2 indicates that the mean levels of female founders on the dependent variable are significantly higher than for male founders ($p < 0.05$).

In Table 3, we report the summary statistics and bivariate correlations of the variables in our study. As expected, different formal education variables are negatively associated with the dependent variable, *informal ties*. For instance, founder's formal education is negatively and significantly correlated with *informal ties* ($r = -0.26$, $p < 0.01$). Furthermore, the interaction of the founder's education and gender is negatively and significantly associated with *informal ties* (r= −0.10, p< 0.01). These bivariate results offer preliminary support for hypotheses 1 and 2.

In Table 4, we report the logistic regression results. The results in this Table offer strong support for hypothesis 1. Model 1 is the base model with control and moderating variables. Models 2 and 3 indicate that the effect of formal education on hiring through *informal ties* is negative and statistically significant (p< 0.01). Furthermore, the marginal effects indicated in parentheses below the coefficients in this Table suggests that these effects are economically significant, that is, one unit change in the educational level is associated with approximately 28.3–34.9% decline in the probability that the founder will hire an employee through *informal ties*. This relationship is further documented in Figure 1. Contrary to our expectation in hypothesis 2, the interaction of formal education and founder's young children, in Model 3, is not significant.

Table 4 also reports subsample analyses testing the moderating effects of gender and young children on the entrepreneur's education-informal ties relationship. Model 4 reports results for the female subsample of 261 new ventures, and Model 5 reports findings for the male subsample of 844 new ventures.[4] Comparing Models 4 and 5 shows an interesting result in the direct effect of formal education on *informal ties*. Though the coefficients of formal education in both models are statistically significant ($p < 0.01$), the marginal effect of one unit change in the educational level is associated with a 58.1% decline in the probability of *informal ties* in the female subsample (Model 4), compared to 25.4% decline in the probability of *informal ties* for the male founder subsample (Model 5). This more nuanced finding related to hypothesis 1 is interesting because it suggests that the marginal benefit of formal education for female entrepreneurs is comparatively more than their male counterparts.

Next, we evaluate and find support for between gender differences highlighted in hypothesis 3, which states that the impact of education on hiring through informal ties or *man-know-man* will be lower for female founders with young children than for their male counterparts. As expected, the marginal effect of the interaction between formal education and young children for the female subsample is positive and significant (marginal effect = 0.543, p< 0.05) (see Table 4). This interaction term is not significant for the male subsample, suggesting that having young children does not affect male entrepreneurs. Figure 2 shows the striking contrast in these effects between the female and the male founders' sub-sample. Overall, these results are consistent with prevailing gender stereotypes related to women's role in families in traditionalist societies. They are also congruent with the view of gender as something that is "done" rather than "is" (e.g. Justo et al., 2015).

4.2. Robustness tests

We conducted additional robustness checks to ensure the consistency of our results. First, we considered alternate measures of the independent variable by using dummy variables

---

[4]We note that nine observations dropped out from the modeling of the female subsample, thereby reducing this subsample from 270 to 261. These nine observations of female entrepreneurs, which are from one state (i.e. Bauchi state) predicted the dependent variable, informal ties perfectly. A recent USAID report shows that in Bauchi state, girls are more vulnerable (i.e. high probability of negative outcome) than boys when they are with their immediate and extended family (i.e. 23.9% vs. 14.2%, and 25.6% vs. 18.2% respectively), accessed http://pdf.usaid.gov/pdf_docs/PA00MQV1.pdf, January 6, 2018. This may help explain the lack of variation in the dependent variable for the female subsample in this particular state.

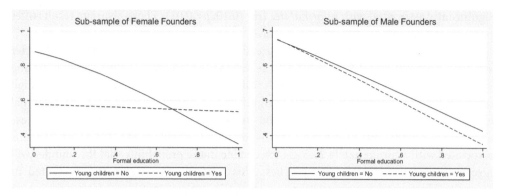

FIGURE 2 Gender Differences in the Predicted Effect of Education.

to measure the extent to which the founders have attained different levels of education (Note that these are the alternate explanatory variables used in the T-tests in Table 2; Coleman & Robb, 2009). The results using these dummy variables in logistic regressions are outlined in Table 5. These results show an interesting pattern which suggests that the variance in hiring through informal ties is more evident in comparatively, lower levels of formal education (i.e. secondary school, and vocational school) as opposed to higher levels of formal education (i.e. university education). Furthermore, the results using this alternate variable show interesting gender differences. That is, whereas the effect of secondary education is negative and insignificant for female founders, it is negative and significant for male founders (marginal effect = −0.133, $p < 0.01$). Similarly, though the effect of vocational education is negative and insignificant for female founders, it is negative and significant for male founders (marginal effect = −0.156, $p < 0.01$). Prima facie, these findings suggest that our primary measure of formal education, which accounts for both the context of education and the educational distribution among both male and female in a given population (see Gimeno et al., 1997) may be a more nuanced construct than dummy variable measures, which only account for context but not the distribution.

Second, we checked for the sensitivity of our results when potentially correlated variables such as firm size (i.e. firm revenues), state fixed effects, and industry effects were excluded. We tried alternative specifications for our models including Probit and simultaneous equation models to account for the potential correlated error structures involving our dependent variable. The results of these robustness checks are consistent with the main results. Together, the results reported above suggest that entrepreneurs' educational attainment in Nigerian ventures is negatively associated with hiring through *informal ties*, and that there are nontrivial, between and within, gender differences in these effects.

5. Discussion

While scholars have examined how entrepreneurship activity varies across different institutional contexts (Busenitz, Gomez, & Spencer, 2000; Kostova, 1997), little attention has been paid to the ways in which the institutional context affects how entrepreneurs mobilize human capital. Building on a context where the practice of hiring through informal ties is commonplace, and often due to a lack of formal institutions supporting

TABLE 5 Robustness Checks Using Alternate Measures of Formal Education.

	Model 6	Model 7	Model 8	Model 9	Model 10	Model 11	Model 12	Model 13
	Female_founded	Male_founded	Female_founded	Male_founded	Female_founded	Male_founded	Female_founded	Male_founded
Secondary school dummy	−0.351 [0.330]	−0.685*** (−0.133) [0.168]						
Vocational school dummy			−0.441 [0.314]	−0.811*** (−0.156) [0.169]				
Bachelor's degree dummy					−0.677 [0.726]	−0.901 [0.575]		
Graduate degree dummy							−1.505 [1.059]	−0.856 [1.071]
Founder's young	−0.435 [0.296]	−0.093 [0.169]	−0.434 [0.297]	−0.124 [0.170]	−0.442 [0.296]	−0.105 [0.167]	−0.437 [0.297]	−0.118 [0.167]
Children (Y = 1)	−1.026** [0.422]	−0.353 [0.220]	−1.014** [0.429]	−0.334 [0.220]	−1.043** [0.424]	−0.309 [0.225]	−1.037** [0.425]	−0.313 [0.222]
Founder's industry experience†	−0.224 [0.219]	−0.390*** [0.113]	−0.217 [0.217]	−0.400*** [0.114]	−0.217 [0.219]	−0.408*** [0.113]	−0.224 [0.218]	−0.416*** [0.113]
Founder's age	−0.291** [0.118]	−0.339*** [0.062]	−0.280** [0.117]	−0.338*** [0.062]	−0.287** [0.121]	−0.386*** [0.060]	−0.304** [0.120]	−0.394*** [0.060]
Firm size†	−0.220 [0.486]	−0.313 [0.259]	−0.232 [0.490]	−0.374 [0.259]	−0.203 [0.494]	−0.364 [0.264]	−0.211 [0.494]	−0.354 [0.260]
Firm age†	1.546 [1.001]	0.014 [0.490]	1.695* [0.977]	0.011 [0.505]	1.492 [0.983]	−0.094 [0.491]	1.492 [0.985]	−0.075 [0.493]
Sole proprietorship	6.777*** [1.898]	7.682*** [1.038]	6.558*** [1.887]	7.673*** [1.040]	6.475*** [1.958]	8.191*** [1.021]	6.736*** [1.931]	8.317*** [1.025]
Industry effects	Yes	Yes	Yes	Yes	Yes	Yes	Yes	Yes
State effects	Yes	Yes	Yes	Yes	Yes	Yes	Yes	Yes
Observations (df_m)	261 (19)	844 (21)	261 (19)	844 (21)	261 (19)	844 (21)	261 (19)	844 (21)
Loglikelihood	−145.1	−480.3	−144.8	−477.8	−145.4	−487.2	−145.2	−488.3
Pseudo R-squared	0.177	0.176	0.179	0.18	0.175	0.164	0.176	0.162
Chi-squared	50.49***	158.3***	51.70***	158.5***	51.20***	145.8***	50.48***	147.5***

*** p < 0.01, ** p < 0.05, * p < 0.1 using two-tailed tests. Marginal effects are in parentheses and bold font. Robust standard errors are in square brackets.

entrepreneurs' access to human capital, we sought not only to highlight the importance of the institutional context in resource mobilization, but also, and more importantly, to understand what drives entrepreneurial agency to rely on informal institutions or, conversely, to deviate from them. Specifically, we examined the influence of general human capital factors (education and gender) on hiring tendencies in new ventures in Nigeria and considered the tension between traditionalist forces such as the *man-know-man* practice (i.e. the tendency to use one's connections to gain access to valuable resources, and segregated gender roles), against modernist forces in the form of formal education in the Nigerian entrepreneurship context.

Our robust findings suggest education is a powerful force restraining entrepreneurs' use of traditional, informal, practices such as the *man-know-man*, thus resulting in a considerably increased reliance on formal institutional practices instead. We further find that though gender moderates this phenomenon, it does so in a manner contrary to predictions from extant literature when using the Gimeno et al. (1997) measure of educational attainment. Though existing theory suggests gender stereotypes would attenuate the effect of formal education on *man-know-man* practice for female entrepreneurs (Igwe, Odunukan, et al., 2020; Jennings & Brush, 2013; Madichie, 2011), we do not find direct evidence to support this claim. Rather, we show that the effect of formal education on deviating from the norms of *man-know-man* practice is twice as much for the female subsample when compared to the male subsample. There are two potential explanations for this interesting but preliminary finding.

First, prior research has indicated that female entrepreneurs have a higher disposition than male entrepreneurs toward democratic-style leadership and lower psychological ownership of their ventures (Justo et al., 2015). Thus, it is possible that more educated female entrepreneurs are able to leverage this disposition toward greater formalization of hiring processes, in an effort to distribute control of the venture among other professionals. But this could also be an attempt to manage their time, given the tendency for female entrepreneurs to multitask between professional and family responsibilities (Arraiz, 2018).

Second, educationally advanced, female entrepreneurs could face an additional driving force to extricate themselves from the traditional binding logic of *man-know-man* in a society that often favors male entrepreneurs. This motivation to deviate from the norm, for highly educated female entrepreneurs could also be a result of the relatively low proportion of female graduates who venture into entrepreneurship (see Owualah, 1999). Also, see Appendix A for a tabulation of the distribution of our sample by gender and education, which supports this notion. Therefore, the minority of women entrepreneurs who are highly educated may be less willing to accept the normative expectations that women should sacrifice their professional careers for their families. In addition, we note that this finding is also consistent with the view that women who decide to become entrepreneurs may be, on average, more adept than their male counterparts (Bardasi et al., 2011). Nevertheless, our findings show that the entrepreneur's family situation (i.e. younger children in the family) activates traditional gender differences in a manner that undermines the potential gains from formal education for female entrepreneurs. Thus, our findings extend recent work on resource mobilization processes in emerging economies in general (e.g. Vissa, 2012), and in Sub-Saharan ventures in particular (e.g., Khayesi & George, 2011) by incorporating the roles of formal education and gender in human resource mobilization. Our findings demonstrate that more educated entrepreneurs in emerging economies have a higher likelihood of deviating from societal norms. This result suggests that the extent of adoption of formal education might have a meaningful impact on the degree of family involvement in new ventures in Sub-Saharan Africa.

Moreover, our findings provide some initial answers to the call for more research in entrepreneurial resource mobilization that focuses on nonfinancial resources, and on the processes via which resources are assembled (Clough et al., 2019). We elucidate human capital drivers and the boundary conditions of entrepreneurial agency in the resource mobilization process in emerging economies. By highlighting the interaction of gender and family situational constraints on the formal education and human resource mobilization relationship, we also contribute to recent discussions that demonstrate the value of a gendered view of entrepreneurship (e.g. Jennings & Brush, 2013; Justo et al., 2015).

6. Conclusion, implications and limitations

6.1. Implications for entrepreneurs

The findings of this research provide some insights to entrepreneurs about the forces that undergird the mobilization of human capital in new ventures. By highlighting the role of education in entrepreneurial resource mobilization in a *man-know-man* society, we demonstrate the viability of formal education in creating alternative pathways for resource mobilization in a context where entrepreneurs often rely on family and friends because they have limited formal institutional alternatives. In particular, we join and extend prior research indicating that investment in general human capital has implications for entrepreneurs' perception of foregone costs of staying in a marginal business (Becker, 1985; Gimeno et al., 1997). In the Sub-Saharan African context, more educated entrepreneurs are likely to move toward more formal processes for hiring in order to enhance the potential of their business. This is particularly true with female entrepreneurs but less so for female entrepreneurs with young children. Future research is needed to further tease out the reasons for these differences. While recent research suggests differences in the way institutions interact with female and male entrepreneurs (Kanze et al., 2018), these differences have not been investigated in emerging economies. Furthermore, it may be that in traditionalist emerging societies, reducing the effects of restraining forces may be even more powerful than in more developed societies with strong formal institutional systems.

Our evidence further demonstrates that more highly educated female entrepreneurs are more sensitive to the impact of younger children than their male counterparts. This has many implications for society and policymakers as well as for female entrepreneurs and their families. While society can help to create change through macro-level institutional Lewin (1947, 1951) purports that it is important to understand what forces will need to be restrained in order to create positive change. Family members of female entrepreneurs, considering our evidence may do well to support them in their efforts to accomplish their informal and professional goals. Given Nigeria's current stage of economic development (Radwan & Pellegrini, 2010), family members ought to provide instrumental support (e.g. assisting with childcare responsibilities) that can help alleviate pressures on female entrepreneurs (Welsh, Kaciak, & Thongpapanl, 2016).

6.2. Implications for public policy

Entrepreneurship is key to a society's economic development, especially in relation to its potential to create jobs. Nigeria, as indicative of many developing countries based on a *man-know-man* culture, is characterized by a high level of nepotistic and corollary corrupt behaviors (Gedajlovic, Carney, Chrisman, & Kellermanns, 2012). While the *man-know-man* practice has the main advantage of providing nascent entrepreneurs' access to valuable resources, the practice has also been argued to perpetuate nepotism and corruption (Ituma & Simpson, 2009). Our findings suggest that policymakers should take a more nuanced approach in their efforts to promote education and entrepreneurship. First, if education can ameliorate economic development while minimizing a practice that is potentially counterproductive, focusing its resource allocation in educational programs – including entrepreneurial management education – may be an effective means to support a government's anti-corruption policies. Such management-focused education, especially at the tertiary level is likely to yield broader dividends for Nigeria as it seeks to transform into a knowledge economy (Radwan & Pellegrini, 2010).

Second, educational initiatives and incentives need to be sensitive to gender differences in the perception of the burden of undertaking education and entrepreneurial activity. Since female entrepreneurs may be under undue pressures from their stereotypical gender roles, which sometimes pushes them to "double work" (Arraiz, 2018; Moult & Anderson, 2005), public policy in support of family-friendly programs for female entrepreneurs may help alleviate some of these pressures. For example, policymakers in developing economies should support business incubators and accelerators' programs toward offering childcare (see Welsh et al., 2016) and school transportation benefits for their participants, as a means to alleviating family pressures on female entrepreneurs that have younger children. Considering that some existing incubators in Nigeria are owned and supported by the government, the government could utilize these incubators to pilot such programs. In a region where female entrepreneurs participate in job creation, and formal entrepreneurial activity is relatively low, developing such family-friendly, entrepreneurial programs can help bolster the success and well-being of female entrepreneurs (and their families) who are struggling to juggle professional career and family life. Gains from such programs are likely to spillover to the broader economy, as well.

6.3. Limitations

Despite the significance of these findings, there are certain limitations in the current analysis that offers useful opportunities for future research. First, the empirical analysis of this paper focuses on a single country context. Future studies can leverage data across different country contexts where reliance on informal ties is highly institutionalized to further delineate the dynamics of resource mobilization in such contexts. Such analyses can offer useful cross-cultural insights related to differences across countries within the region, while elaborating on intervening mechanisms that either accentuate or diminish this tension between formal and informal institutional forces.

Second, our proxy for informal ties in this context is based primarily on a random measure of how the new venture hired their most recent employee. As such, our inferences about empirical regularities are based on a single observation for each venture in our sample. While the findings indicate robust support for the hypotheses, we were unable to tease out within venture variance in hiring patterns. Thus, future studies can focus on using qualitative data to provide a more nuanced account of the internal moderators that contribute to within-ventures variance in hiring patterns. This can enhance our understanding of firm mechanisms that contribute to entrepreneurial resource mobilization.

Third, our interest in this initial analysis was to understand the role of general human capital factors, such as education and gender, in influencing the institutional norms in a weak institutional context, that is, in a context where formal institutions are often deficient. In the interest of precision, we have paid less attention to other individual-level forces that could also impact this framework. For example, even though we controlled for industry-specific human capital in our models, we have not theorized about its possible role in this framework. We encourage future research that can extend the current study by considering the role of industry-specific experience in this framework, and the associated boundary conditions imposed by industry characteristics.

Acknowledgements

We acknowledge helpful feedback from seminar participants at the Strategic Management Society, and the Academy of Management on earlier drafts of this paper. We thank the World Bank Group for providing access to the dataset used in this research, "*Enterprise Surveys (http://www.enterprisesurveys.org), The World Bank Group*". Any opinions and conclusions expressed herein are those of the authors and do not necessarily represent the views of the World Bank. Every effort has been made to protect the confidentiality of the data in accordance with World Bank rules governing "strictly confidential" information.

Disclosure statement

No potential conflict of interest was reported by the authors.

References

Acquaah, M. (2012). Social networking relationships, firm-specific managerial experience, and firm performance in a transition economy: A comparative analysis of family owned and nonfamily firms. *Strategic Management Journal*, 33, 1215–1228.

Ahlstrom, D., & Bruton, G. D. (2006). Venture capital in emerging economies: Networks and institutional change. *Entrepreneurship Theory & Practice*, 30(2), 299–320.

Aldrich, H. E., & Cliff, J. E. (2003). The pervasive effects of family on entrepreneurship: Toward a family embeddedness perspective. *Journal of Business Venturing*, 18, 573–596.

Amankwah-Amoah, J., Ifere, S. E., & Nyuur, R. B. (2016). Human capital and strategic persistence: An examination of underperforming workers in two emerging economies. *Journal of Business Research*, 69, 4348–4357.

Amine, L. S., & Staub, K. M. (2009). Women entrepreneurs in sub-Saharan Africa: An institutional theory analysis from a social marketing point of view'. *Entrepreneurship & Regional Development*, 21(2), 183–211.

Aragon-Mendoza, J., Pardo Del Val, M., & Roig-Dobon, S. (2016). The influence of institutions development in venture creation decision: A cognitive view. *Journal of Business Research*, 69, 4941–4946.

Arraiz, I. (2018). Time to share the load: Gender differences in household responsibilities and business profitability. *Small Business Economics*, 51, 57–84.

Arregle, J.-L., Batjargal, B., Hitt, M. A., Webb, J. W., Miller, T., & Tsui, A. S. (2013). Family ties in entrepreneurs' social networks and new venture growth. *Entrepreneurship Theory and Practice*, 39(2), 313–344.

Azolukwan, V. A., & Perkins, S. J. (2009). Managerial perspectives on HRM in Nigeria: Evolving hybridization? *Cross Cultural Management: An International Journal*, 16(1), 62–82.

Bardasi, E., Sabarwal, S., & Terrell, K. (2011). How do female entrepreneurs perform? Evidence from three developing regions. *Small Business Economics*, 37, 417–441.

Becker, G. S. (1985). Human capital, effort, and the sexual division of labor. *Journal of Labor Economics*, 3(1), S33–S58.

Brüderl, J., Preisendorfer, P., & Ziegler, R. (1992). Survival chances of newly founded business organizations. *American Sociological Review*, 57(2), 227–242.

Brush, C. G. (1992). Research on women business owners: Past trends, a new perspective and future directions'. *Entrepreneurship Theory and Practice*, 16(4), 5–30.

Busenitz, L. W., Gomez, C., & Spencer, J. W. (2000). Country institutional profiles: Interlocking entrepreneurial phenomena. *Academy of Management Journal*, 43, 994–1003.

Carraher, S. M., Welsh, D. H. B., & Svilokos, A. (2016). Validation of a measure of social entrepreneurship. *European Journal of International Management*, 10(4), 386–402.

Casper, W. J., Harris, C., Taylor-Bianco, A., & Wayne, J. H. (2011). Work-family conflict, perceived supervisor support and organizational commitment among Brazilian professionals. *Journal of Vocational Behavior*, 79(3), 640–652.

Chang, K. (2011). A path to understanding guanxi in China's transitional economy: Variations on network behavior. *Sociological Theory*, 29, 315–339.

Clough, D. R., Fang, T. P., Vissa, B., & Wu, A. (2019). Turning lead into gold: How do entrepreneurs mobilize resources to exploit opportunities? *Academy of Management Annals*, 13(1), 240–271.

Coleman, S., & Robb, A. (2009). A comparison of new firm financing by gender: Evidence from the Kaffman Firm Survey data. *Small Business Economics*, 33, 397–411.

Cooper, A. C., Gimeno-Gascon, F. J., & Woo, C. Y. (1994). Initial human and financial capital as predictors of new venture performance. *Journal of Business Venturing*, 9, 371–395.

Cruz, C., Justo, R., & De Castro, J. O. (2012). 'Does family employment enhance MSEs performance? Integrating socioemotional wealth and family embeddedness perspectives'. *Journal of Business Venturing*, 27, 62–76.

Cuervo-Cazurra, A., Gaur, A., & Singh, D. (2019). Pro-market institutions and global strategy: The pendulum of pro-market reforms and reversal. *Journal of International Business Studies*, 50, 598–612.

Davis, A. E., & Shaver, K. G. (2012). Understanding gendered variations in business growth intentions across the life course. *Entrepreneurship Theory & Practice*, 36(3), 495–512.

Dimova, R., & Pela, K. (2018). Entrepreneurship: Structural transformation, skills, and constraints. *Small Business Economics*, 51, 203–220.

Ding, W. W. (2011). The impact of founders' professional-education background on the adoption of open science by for-profit biotechnology firms. *Management Science*, 57(2), 257–273.

Ezema, B. I., & Ogujiuba, K. (2012). The development state debate: Where is Nigeria? *Journal of Sustainable Development*, 5(1), 100–113.

Fairlie, R. W., & Robb, A. M. (2009). Gender differences in business performance: Evidence from the characteristics of business owners survey. *Small Business Economics*, 33, 375–395.

Fajana, S., Owoyemi, O., Elegbede, T., & Gbajumo-Sheriff, M. (2011). Human resource management practices in Nigeria. *Journal of Management and Strategy*, 2(2), 57–62.

Fukuyama, F. (2009). Westernization versus modernization. *New Perspectives Quarterly*, 26, 84–89.

Gedajlovic, E., Carney, M., Chrisman, J. J., & Kellermanns, F. W. (2012). The adolescence of family firm research: Taking stock and planning for the future. *Journal of Management*, 38(4), 1010–1037.

Gimeno, J., Folta, T. B., Cooper, A. C., & Woo, C. Y. (1997). Survival of the fittest? Entrepreneurial human capital and the persistence of underperforming firms. *Administrative Science Quarterly*, 42(4), 750–783.

Hack-Polay, D., Igwe, P. A., & Madichie, N. O. (2020). The Role of institutional and family embeddedness in the failure of Sub-Saharan African migrant family businesses. *The International Journal of Entrepreneurship and Innovation*. doi:10.1177/1465750320909732

Hallen, B. L. (2008). The causes and consequences of the initial network positions of new organizations: From whom do entrepreneurs receive investments? *Administrative Science Quarterly*, 53(4), 685–718.

Henry, C., Foss, L., & Ahl, H. (2016). Gender and entrepreneurship research: A review of methodological approaches. *International Small Business Journal*, 34(3), 217–241.

Hofstede, G., & Hofstede, G. J. (2005). *Cultures and organizations: Software of the mind* (Rev. 2nd ed.). New York: McGraw-Hill.

Horak, S. (2017). The informal dimension of human resource management in Korea: Yongo, recruiting practices and career progression. *The International Journal of Human Resource Management*, 28(10), 1409–1432.

Hoskisson, R. E., Eden, L., Lau, C. M., & Wright, M. (2000). Strategy in emerging economies. *Academy of Management Journal*, 43(3), 249–267.

Hsu, D. H. (2007). Experienced entrepreneurial founders, organizational capital, and venture capital funding. *Research Policy*, 36(5), 722–741.

Igwe, P. A., Madichie, N. O., & Amoncar, N. (2020). Transgenerational business legacies and intergenerational succession among the Igbos (Nigeria). *Small Enterprise Research*, 27, 165–179.

Igwe, P. A., Odunukan, K., Rahman, M., Rugara, D. G., & Ochinanwata, C. (2020). How entrepreneurship ecosystem influences the development of frugal innovation and informal entrepreneurship? *Thunderbird International Business Review*, 62(5), 475–488.

Ihugba, O. A., Odii, A., & Njoku, A. (2013). Challenges and prospects of entrepreneurship in Nigeria. *Academic Journal of Interdisciplinary Studies*, 2(5), 25–36.

Inglehart, R. (1991). *Culture shift in advanced industrial society*. Princeton: Princeton University Press.

Inyang, B. J., & Enuoh, R. O. (2009). Entrepreneurial competencies: The missing links to successful entrepreneurship in Nigeria. *International Business Research*, 2(2), 62–71.

Ituma, A., & Simpson, R. (2009). The 'boundaryless' career and career boundaries: Applying an institutionalist perspective to ICT workers in the context of Nigeria. *Human Relations*, 62(5), 727–761.

Jackson, T. (2004). *Management and change in Africa: A cross-cultural perspective*. London, UK: Routledge.

Jennings, J. E., & Brush, C. G. (2013). Research on women entrepreneurs: Challenges to (and from) the broader entrepreneurship literature. *Academy of Management Annals*, 7(1), 663–715.

Jennings, J. E., & McDougald, M. S. (2007). Work–family interface experiences and coping strategies: Implications for entrepreneurship research and practice. *Academy of Management Review*, 32(3), 747–760.

Justo, R., Detienne, D. R., & Sieger, P. (2015). Failure or voluntary exit? Reassessing the female underperformance hypothesis. *Journal of Business Venturing*, 30, 775–792.

Kanze, D., Huang, L., Conley, M. A., & Higgins, E. T. (2018). We ask men to win and women not to lose: Closing the gender gap in startup funding. *Academy of Management Journal*, 61(2), 586–614.

Khayesi, J. N. O., & George, G. (2011). When does the socio-cultural context matter? Communal orientation and entrepreneurs' resource accumulation efforts in Africa. *Journal of Occupational and Organizational Psychology, 84*, 471–492.

Khayesi, J. N. O., George, G., & Antonakis, J. (2014). Kinship in entrepreneur networks: Performance effects of resource assembly in Africa. *Entrepreneurship Theory & Practice, 38*, 1323–1342.

Kostova, T. (1997). Country institutional profiles: Concepts and measurement. In *Proceedings of the Academy of Management* (pp. 180–185). Briarcliff Manor, NY: Academy of Management.

Kotha, R., & George, G. (2012). Friends, family, or fools: Entrepreneurial experience and its implications for equity distribution and resource mobilization. *Journal of Business Venturing, 27*(5), 525–543.

Lewin, K. (1947). Group decision and social change. In T. M. Newcomb, E. L. Hartley (Eds.), *Readings in social psychology* (pp. 330–344). New York: Harper.

Lewin, K. (1951). *Field theory in social science: Selected theoretical papers* (D. Cartwright, Ed.). New York: Harper & Row.

Liu, X. X., Keller, J., & Hong, Y. Y. (2014). Hiring of personal ties: A cultural consensus analysis of China and the United States. *Management and Organization Review, 11*(1), 145–169.

Luo, Y., Huang, Y., & Wang, S. L. (2012). Guanxi and organizational performance: A meta-analysis. *Management and Organization Review, 8*(1), 139–172.

Madichie, N. O. (2009). Breaking the glass ceiling in Nigeria: A review of women's entrepreneurship. *Journal of African Business, 10*(1), 51–66.

Madichie, N. O. (2011). Setting an agenda for women entrepreneurship in Nigeria: A commentary on Faseke's journey through time for the Nigerian woman. *Gender in Management: An International Journal, 26*(3), 212–219.

Moult, S., & Anderson, A. R. (2005). Enterprising women: Gender and maturity in new venture creation and development. *Journal of Enterprising Culture, 13*(3), 255–271.

Nafziger, E. W. (1969). The effect of the Nigerian extended family on entrepreneurial activity. *Economic Development and Cultural Change, 18*, 25–33.

Ncube, M., Soonawalla, K., & Hausken, K. (2019). The links between business environment, economic growth and social equity: A study of African countries. *Journal of African Business*, 1–24. doi:10.1080/15228916.2019.1695184

North, D. (1990). *Institutions, institutional change and economic performance*. Cambridge, UK: Cambridge University Press.

Owualah, S. I. (1999). Banks and consultants in Nigeria's job creation program. *Small Business Economics, 12*, 321–330.

Peng, M. W., Sun, S. L., Pinkham, B., & Chen, H. (2009). The institution-based view as a third leg for a strategy tripod. *Academy of Management Perspectives, 23*(4), 63–81.

Peng, M. W., Wang, D. Y. L., & Jiang, Y. (2008). An institution-based view of international business strategy: A focus on emerging economies. *Journal of International Business Studies, 39*, 920–936.

Radwan, I., & Pellegrini, G. (2010). *Knowledge, productivity, and innovation in Nigeria*. Washington, DC: The World Bank. Retrieved from http://siteresources.worldbank.org/INTRANETTRADE/Resources/239054-1239120299171/5998577-1254498644362/6461208-1300202947570/Nigeria_ICT.pdf

United Nations. (2017a, December 17). *World population prospects 2017*. Retrieved from https://esa.un.org/unpd/wpp/DataQuery/

United Nations. (2017b, December 17). *World population projected to reach 9.8 billion in 2050*. Retrieved from http://www.un.org/en/development/desa/population/events/pdf/other/21/21June_FINAL%20PRESS%20RELEASE_WPP17.pdf

Vissa, B. (2012). Agency in action: Entrepreneurs' networking style and initiation of economic exchange. *Organization Science, 23*(2), 492–510.

Welsh, D. H. B., Kaciak, E., & Shamah, R. (2018). Determinants of women entrepreneurs' firm performance in a hostile environment. *Journal of Business Research, 88*, 481–491.

Welsh, D. H. B., Kaciak, E., & Thongpapanl, N. (2016). Influence of stages of economic development on women entrepreneurs' startups. *Journal of Business Research, 69*, 4933–4940.

Williams, D. R. (2004). Effects of childcare activities on duration of self-employment in Europe. *Entrepreneurship Theory and Practice, 28*(5), 467–485.

Woldie, A., & Adersua, A. (2004). Female entrepreneurs in a transitional economy: Businesswomen in Nigeria. *International Journal of Social Economics, 31*(1), 78–93.

World Bank. (2015). *World Bank national accounts data, and OECD national account data files.* Retrieved from http://data.worldbank.org/indicator/NY.GDP.PCAP.CD

World Bank. (2017). *The World Bank Data – Nigeria.* Retrieved from https://data.worldbank.org/country/nigeria

World Bank. (2020a, December 4). *Education statistics: Gross enrollment ratio, secondary.* Retrieved from https://datatopics.worldbank.org/education/indicators

World Bank. (2020b, December 4). *Data for Sub-Saharan Africa, Nigeria.* Retrieved from https://data.worldbank.org/indicator/NY.GDP.PCAP.CD?locations=NG

APPENDIX A

Distribution of Study Sample by Educational Attainment and Gender.

Educational Attainment	Female_founded	Male_founded	Total	% Female_founded
Lower than Secondary School	110	427	537	20.48
Secondary School	57	102	159	35.85
Vocational School	43	99	142	30.28
Some University Training	51	192	243	20.99
Bachelor's degree	6	21	27	22.22
Graduate degree	3	6	9	33.33

ᗺ OPEN ACCESS

How to Start an African Informal Entrepreneurial Revolution?

Paul Agu Igwe [iD] and Chinedu Ochinanwata

ABSTRACT
The achievement of business sustainability is dependent on the interacting components of the entrepreneurship ecosystem (EE) and institutions that support or challenge the business environment. Given the importance of the informal economy in developing economies, we need to rethink how to start an informal entrepreneurial revolution. This article examines the nexus of the informal entrepreneurial ecosystem, from the perspective of ecological resilience. Specifically, the article analyzes the significant differences between the formal sector, the informal sector, frugal innovations, and the supportive ecosystem resilience that produces unparalleled enthusiasm. Conceptually, this article developed propositions and a model of Productive and Unproductive EE explaining the business environment and the interacting predictors from the African regional context. Arguably, as entrepreneurial education and skills increases, there is more likelihood of the creation of formal ventures and growth-oriented micro, small and medium enterprises (MSMEs). These have implications for economic growth and – in the case of African economies – moving the informal to formal economy.

Introduction

Entrepreneurship ecosystem (EE) consist of interacting components and actors, which foster new firm creation and growth-oriented activities (Brown & Mason, 2017; Mack & Mayer, 2015; Maroufkhani, Wagner, Khairuzzaman, & Ismail, 2018). Isenberg (2010, 2011) proposes that EE enables or hinders entrepreneurship development, growth, and productivity. In many African countries, the informal sector is a major contributor to the national economy, accounting for a significant portion of employment and between 25% and 65% of GDP (International Monetary Fund [IMF], 2017). Informal economy helps to create jobs, spur innovation, and reduce inequality by generating employment opportunities for minorities and disadvantaged groups (like youths and women in developing countries). However, little attention has been paid to the role of entrepreneurship in fostering economic growth in African economies (African Development Bank [ADB], 2013; Madichie, Hinson, & Ibrahim, 2013; Rwelamila & Ssegawa, 2014). A major challenge is how to move the informal sector to a formal economy, achieve efficient resource allocation and high output (Kim & Loayza, 2017; World Economic Forum, 2015).

This is an Open Access article distributed under the terms of the Creative Commons Attribution License (http://creativecommons.org/licenses/by/4.0/), which permits unrestricted use, distribution, and reproduction in any medium, provided the original work is properly cited.

EE influences the growth of entrepreneurship across locations, regions, and nations (Block, Fisch, & van Praag, 2017; Fishman, Don-Yehiya, & Schreiber, 2018). In the Global Entrepreneurship Monitor (GEM studies), Africa displays the highest levels of entrepreneurial intention (42%) while Latin America and the Caribbean (LAC) report the highest capability perception (63%) and the second-highest rate of entrepreneurial intention (32%) (GEM, 2016/2017). The same pattern is observed in terms of societal value for entrepreneurship and capabilities perceptions (Mahoney & Michael, 2005). GEM report revealed that from a regional perspective, Africa shows the most positive attitudes toward entrepreneurship, with three-quarters of working-age adults considering entrepreneurship a good career choice while 77% believe that entrepreneurs are admired in their societies (GEM, 2016/2017). However, when it comes to nascent entrepreneurial activity (those who go on to commit resources to start a formal business), the African region lack behind LAC (GEM, 2016/2017).

A major question of this article is how to start an informal entrepreneurial revolution? Ecological resilience describes an ecosystem that can "absorb" disturbances and undergo the changes necessary to transform its essential behaviors, structures, and identity into a system that is better able to respond to disruptions (Roundy, Brockman, & Bradshaw, 2017). It is assumed that each ecosystem should be specific and idiosyncratic (Sheriff & Muffatto, 2015). EE has a significant influence on both the formal and informal economy, firms' productivity, and level of entrepreneurship (Mathias, Solomon, & Madison, 2017). In the case of Africa, the majority of the population pursue entrepreneurial intentions but rather in the informal and low productive business activities (International Labor Organization [ILO], 2014). With a focus on the African economy, this article proposes strengthening the EE to support informal entrepreneurship, firm productivity, and growth-oriented productive entrepreneurship.

This is one of the foremost studies to draw on ecosystem resilience to analyze the African informal economy. Most entrepreneurship studies focus on the formal economy. Unfortunately, the increasing interest in formal entrepreneurship has left the informal economy under-researched (Freire-Gibb & Nielsen, 2014). Therefore, this article contributes to knowledge on the main determinants of productivity linked to the EE from a developing regional context. Lack of specification and conceptual limitations has undoubtedly hindered our understanding of EE from different contexts (Brown & Mason, 2017; Mason & Brown, 2014; Stam & Van De Ven, 2019). Also, this article contributes to defining EE, since it remains loosely defined (Brown & Mason, 2017). More so, this paper contributes to describing frugal innovations and the institutional perspectives of a challenging environment (Welter & Smallbone, 2011). Understanding institutional elements could form a solid base for the formulation of enabling supports and policies directed toward entrepreneurial revolution (Isenberg, 2010). Above all, an improved understanding of the EE has policy implications toward job creation, economic growth, innovation, and – in the case of African economies – poverty reduction, and the potential to formalize the informal sector (Kuckertz, 2019).

Although this study's focus on informal entrepreneurship, most of the discussions also affect the formal entrepreneurship sector. The article is structured as follows: The next section examines the foundational theories of EE and ecological resilience, informal entrepreneurship, frugal innovations, and institutional logics. This is followed by the development of propositions and a model of Productive and Unproductive EE. Finally, the article concludes with an analysis of the critical challenges and implications for growth-oriented entrepreneurship, research, practice, and policy.

Entrepreneurship ecosystem and ecological resilience

An evolutionary concept of EE explains the factors of the surrounding environment that support or hinder entrepreneurship growth (Roundy, 2017; Sheriff & Muffatto, 2015). EE model consists of six main elements that are Policy, Finance, Culture, Supports, Human Capital and Markets (Isenberg, 2011). Within these six domains, there are several hundreds of elements interacting in highly complex and idiosyncratic ways (Isenberg, 2014). The evolving ecosystem consists of actors that govern, integrate, and perform all of the functions required for entrepreneurship to flourish in any territory that becomes an important source of innovation, productivity growth and source of employment (Stam & Van De Ven, 2019). EE approach has been adopted in many studies (Brown & Mason, 2017; Maroufkhani et al., 2018; Stam & Van De Ven, 2019). Despite its popularity, the definitions are varied (Brown & Mason, 2017). It remains loosely defined and measured; hence, requires definitional clarification (Table 1).

EE offers both a theoretical and practical perspective (Beliaeva, Ferasso, Kraus, & Damke, 2020; Brown & Mason, 2017; Stam & Van De Ven, 2019). Although the idea of EE and its application somehow has been embraced by researchers and policymakers, some scholars caution that the concept should be treated with care, as the metaphor risks being vague and its boundaries blurry (Bruns, Bosma, Sanders, & Schramm, 2017; Kuckertz, 2019). EE is known to produce informal, formal, productive, and unproductive entrepreneurship depending on the interreacting factors. Ecological resilience or ecological robustness describes the ability of an ecosystem to maintain its normal patterns of

Table 1. Definitions of entrepreneurial ecosystem.

Author/Year	Definitions
Saúde et al. (2020)	A territorial area/space including a variety of institutional and individual actors that foster and support the entrepreneurial spirit, innovation and entrepreneurship, in a coordinated way.
Kuckertz (2019)	A regional, complex agglomeration of entrepreneurial activity providing two classes of relevant services, namely (a) enhanced entrepreneurial activity benefiting its larger economic and societal environment and (b) various forms of formal and informal support that enhance the probability of success of the entrepreneurial activity.
Pereira et al. (2019)	A system composed of a range of stakeholders, public and private, individual and collective, as well as the full set of policy measures defined and adopted to enhance their action, articulation, and co-development, to promote entrepreneurship, value creation, and economic development.
Shwetzer, Maritz, and Nguyen (2019)	A set of interconnected entrepreneurial actors, organizations, institutions and entrepreneurial processes, which formally and informally coalesce to connect, mediate and govern the performance within the local entrepreneurial environment, involving a dynamic and systemic nature, within a supportive environment.
Stam and Van De Ven (2019)	Consists of all the interdependent actors and factors that enable and constrain entrepreneurship within a particular territory.
Acs, Audretsch, Lehmann, and Licht (2016)	An ecosystem consists of exogenously given components, the environment, and agents acting endogenously together as a system, linked by generating benefits from the interrelationship.

Source: Compiled by Authors

nutrient cycling and biomass production after being subjected to damage caused by an ecological disturbance (Levin, 2015).

Ecosystem resilience explains the ability of the EE to respond to disruptions that are changing, adapting, and evolving over time. Resilience can be defined as the ability of a system to maintain its state by absorbing both internal and external changes and disturbances to its variables and parameters (Özkundakci & Lehmann, 2019). Over time, the concepts of ecosystem resilience have become prominent in the scientific and management literature (Falk, Watts, & Thode, 2019). Ecosystem resilience applies to post-disturbance response, but resilient responses are emergent properties resulting from component processes of persistence, recovery, and reorganization (Falk et al., 2019). One of the most important concepts related to resilience is the notion that complex systems can exhibit non-equilibrium conditions and exist in various alternative states that differ in processes, structures, functions, and feedbacks (Chambers, Allen, & Cushman, 2019).

Informality and African economy

Different definitions of informality have been used in the literature based on different conceptual understandings related to the size of the firm, size of employees, the legal status of employment, social protection status, tax compliance, etc. For example, Pradhan and van Soest (1997) and Maloney (1999) use definitions classifying firms employing fewer than six employees as informal in their studies of Bolivia and Mexico respectively. The informal sector takes the form of self-employment (often regarded as survival activities for marginalized workers) (Ram, Edwards, Jones, & Villares-Varela, 2017). Other attributes of informality include being unregistered, usually unlicensed, and typically do not pay taxes (Igwe et al., 2020; Igwe, Madichie, & Newbery, 2019). The informal economy does not cover illicit activities but focuses on legal activities (Maloney, 2004; OECD, 2019). A range of alternative definitions of informal activity implying very different conceptual understandings and views are summarized in Table 2.

Table 2. Views and definitions of informal economy.

Definitions of Informality		Sources
All economic activities by workers and economic units that are – in law or practice – not covered or insufficiently covered by formal arrangements.	Legal arrangement	OECD (2019)
Economic sectors and units that are not registered with the state and workers who do not receive social protection through their work, both wage-employed and self-employed.	Legal arrangement	OECD (2017)
Comprises household unincorporated enterprises with informal market products (optionally, all, or those that are not registered under specific forms of national legislation)	Legal arrangement	ILO (1993)
All economic activities by workers and economic units that are – in law or practice – not covered or insufficiently covered by formal arrangements.	Legal arrangement	ILO (2014)
All remunerative work – both self-employment and wage employment – that is not recognized, regulated or protected by existing legal or regulatory frameworks as well as non-remunerative work undertaken in an income-producing enterprise.	Labor market	Chen and Hamori (2009)
Comprises the less advantaged sector of a dualistic or segmented labor market	Labor market	Maloney (2004)

Source: Compiled by Authors.

According to the African Development Bank (ADB, 2013), 9 out of 10 rural and urban workers have informal jobs in Africa and most employees are women and youths. Examples of informal jobs include artisans, market traders, street traders, subsistence farmers, small-scale manufacturers, service providers (e.g. hairdressers, private taxi drivers, and carpenters), etc. It is estimated that more than 60% of the African population in employment is in the informal economy (ILO, 2018; World Bank, 2016). Besides the problem of informality, African economies are characterized by several interacting components, features, and disruptions that are changing, adapting, and evolving (as presented in Table 3).

As revealed by several studies (Table 3), the majority of African economies lack adequate institutional supports for entrepreneurship leading to the ecosystem that produces a high

Table 3. African entrepreneurial ecosystem environment.

Interreacting Factors	Sources
A lack of adequate institutional supports for entrepreneurship	Igwe, Amaugo, Ogundana, Egere, and Anigbo (2018); Ratten and Jones (2018)
Ecosystem produces micro, small and informal enterprises	Nwajiuba, Igwe, Binuomote, Nwajiuba, and Nwekpa (2020a); Igwe (2020)
Low-quality education, low skills and necessity-driven enterprises	Global Entrepreneurship Monitor (GEM, 2014, 2015); Igwe et al., 2019; Okolie et al. (2019)
Adverse ecosystem, unfavorable culture, high rate of corruption and unfavorable regulations	Nwajiuba et al. (2020a); Igwe et al. (2018)
Gender-discriminatory environments, discriminatory social norms, work-to-family conflict and stereotypes	Madichie (2009); McGowan, Cooper, Durkin, & O'Kane, 2015; Okolie et al., 2021; Guma (2015); Madichie, Nkamnebe, and Idemobi (2008)
High rate of MSMEs failure and underperformance	Kellermanns, Walter, Crook, Kemmerer, and Narayanan (2016); World Bank (2013)
Culture is a major challenge that has impeded entrepreneurship	Nwajiuba et al. (2020a); Vershinina, Beta, and Murithi (2018); Ezeoha and Icha-Ituma (2017)
Limited evidence-based policy, weak entrepreneurial ecosystem, lack of innovation, research and development	World Bank (2015)
Weak infrastructure (such as power supply and transport network), immature capital markets; poor quality of education	World Economic Forum (2019); Igwe et al. (2018); Igwe et al. (2019)
Low gross domestic product (GDP) per capita, which leads to low demand	World Economic Forum (2019)
Overdependence on materials sourced locally	Ekekwe (2016)
Mobile technology, open-source software and ideas from local technology hubs supporting innovations	Ekekwe (2016)
Dominated by subsistence agriculture and extraction businesses, with a heavy reliance on (unskilled) labor and natural resources	GEM (2018)
Poverty, corruption and dissatisfaction with government policies	Nwajiuba et al. (2020a)
MSMEs lack market information, credit history and collateral required by the traditional lending institutions	Nwajiuba et al. (2020a)
Business loans are usually very limited in volume, have high interest rates, and are mostly short-term	Mwobobia (2012)
Formal financial system services a small proportion of the adult population (e.g. in Nigeria, about 35% of adults)	Igwe et al. (2018)
Terrorist activities such as Boko Haram and Islamic State of West Africa Province (ISWAP) and internal security challenges such as kidnapping, farmers-Fulani herders clashes and armed bandits	Igwe, Ochinanwata, and Madichie (2021)
Smuggling and Informal cross-border trade	Igwe et al. (2021)

Source: Compiled by Authors

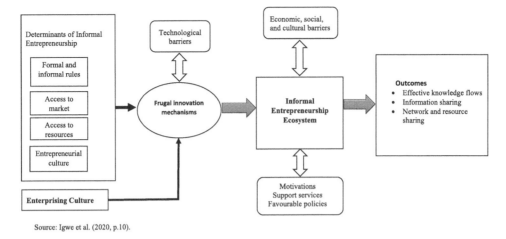

Figure 1. A model of frugal innovation ecosystem. Source: Igwe et al. (2020, p. 10)

rate of informal micro, small, and medium enterprises (MSMEs) which are low growth-oriented. As a result, many economies are over-dependent on locally sourced materials, mobile technology, and local technology hubs supporting frugal innovations (Ekekwe, 2016). Therefore, frugal innovation has emerged as a novel approach toward improving EE (Beliaeva et al., 2020; Igwe et al., 2020; Meagher, 2018). Frugal innovation is the ability to 'do better with fewer resources for more people or the ability to maximize the ratio of value to resources for customers, shareholders, or society (Prabhu, 2017).

Researchers and policymakers are interested in determining whether and to what extent the development and production of so-called frugal innovations contribute to economic development? (see, for example, Meagher, 2018). It is believed that EE provides a rich background for risk-taking, innovative and visionary entrepreneurship, thereby enabling the productive use of limited resources to be better targeted and more focused on optimum returns (Brown & Mason, 2017; Pereira et al., 2019; Saúde, Hermozilha, & Borrero, 2020). Igwe et al. (2020) developed a model of a frugal innovation ecosystem that is dependent on formal/informal rules, access to market, access to resources and entrepreneurial culture (Figure 1).

As shown by the model (Figure 1), frugal innovations and informal entrepreneurship develop in response to technological, economic, social, and cultural barriers that exist in many African economies. Depending on the support services or policies, informal entrepreneurship produces effective knowledge flows, information sharing, networking, and resource sharing. These outcomes or responses provide an ecosystem of resilience, resistance, recovery, and sustainability. It is believed that frugal innovation is fueled by need, the science and art of using the little available resources to solve problems (Thoughtwork, 2014).

Institutional logic

Developing strong institutions is an excellent starting point toward starting an entrepreneurial revolution (Isenberg, 2010). Institutions are formal rules (i.e. laws and regulations) and informal rules (i.e. norms, values, beliefs, religion, etc.) that guide individual behavior (DiMaggio & Powell, 1991; North, 1990). Institutional logics has been applied to explain why the levels of entrepreneurship vary from one location to another (DiMaggio & Powell, 1991; Naudé, 2010). Institutions are maintained through repeated endorsement by individuals engaging in social interactions that become entrenched when people perform the patterns of behavior encrypted in them until any other behavior becomes unthinkable (Seo & Creed, 2002). Culture is directly associated with the informal institution. Informal business practices occur outside of formal regulations and are guided by informal norms, values, and understanding (Sutter, Webb, Kistruck, Ketchen, & Ireland, 2017). Entrepreneurship is inextricably linked to institutions and the sociocultural system (Ajekwu, 2017; Anggadwita, Ramadani, & Ratten, 2017).

Sometimes, the cultural richness of regions is often ignored in economic development initiatives (Mack & Mayer, 2015). This perspective describes how institutional and cultural elements are embedded, become manifest in the actions of individuals and organizational change (Thornton, Ocasio, & Lounsbury, 2012; Williams & Vorley, 2015). High-growth entrepreneurship thrives in favorable economic and institutional environments that enhance the expected returns of innovation (Kim & Loayza, 2017; World Bank, 2014). There have been several studies examining the experiences and lessons from formalization initiatives in developing economies (Abdallah, 2017; Amésquita, Morales, & Rees, 2018; Igwe et al., 2019; Olomi, Charles, & Juma, 2018). Feldman and Lowe (2017) maintain that among institutions, government is arguably the best-equipped actor in the economy to make large-scale investments in infrastructure and education. To promote economic growth, governments often introduce policies and new regulations aimed at promoting entrepreneurship. Often unforeseen outcomes from insufficient regulation can undermine policies designed to promote entrepreneurship and lead to the emergence of informal activities and hidden enterprise culture (Al-Mataani, Wainwright, & Demirel, 2017).

Productive and unproductive entrepreneurial ecosystem

There is a diversity of EE, institutions, and actors. The diversity of EE determines whether an economy develops into the formal or informal sector and productive or unproductive entrepreneurship. The emergence of either sector depends on the nature of the institutional framework described within the EE including policy framework, finance, culture, supports, human capital, and markets. An entrepreneur is a person who identifies a business opportunity, acquires the necessary physical and human capital to start a new venture, and operationalizes it and is responsible for its success or failure. A mapping of the EE illustrates the actors' roles, which indicates their importance and the interconnectedness between them. Understanding institutional logics can provide an appropriate interpretative frame to examine how to start an informal entrepreneurial revolution. Therefore, the emerging EE has several evolving dimensions and propositions.

Proposition 1: Depending on the entrepreneurship ecosystem resilience, productive or unproductive entrepreneurship and the formal or informal economy will dominate.

Depending on EE formal or informal entrepreneurship will emerge and the differences of the two types of ecosystems have important implications for EE resilience. Indeed, EE influence the ease with which entrepreneurs decide either to operate in a formal or informal system. The informal sector has a small layer that responds to the simplification of regulations and a larger one that requires a different formalization framework (Olomi et al., 2018). The formalization of informal firms within the fold of the formal sector has been suggested as the possible solution to poverty reduction in low-income countries (World Bank, 2016).

However, the transition to the formal sector has been notoriously difficult to achieve and slow in most countries. Formal and informal rules are components of institutions that influence the levels of entrepreneurship and variation of entrepreneurship by location, country, regions, etc. Therefore, the institutional setting could be divided into urban and rural. When measured against all indicators, the rural sector is the worst off. As a result, people living in rural areas are almost twice as likely to be in informal employment as those in urban areas and agriculture is the sector with the highest level of informal employment (ILO, 2018).

Proposition 2: As entrepreneurship education and awareness increases, there is more likelihood of the creation of formal ventures and growth-oriented entrepreneurship.

Among the critical resources required to develop a productive economy is quality education. One of the debates in the current society is can entrepreneurship be learned or can people be trained and motivated to develop entrepreneurial intentions (Igwe, Okolie, & Nwokoro, 2021; Okolie et al., 2021). There is consensus that entrepreneurship education and the development of employability skills and knowledge contributes to making an individual adapt to changes in the labor market (Igwe, Lock, & Rugara, 2020). As an economy grows it requires skilled entrepreneurs and labor. Sustainable development at all levels in society requires reorienting education and helping people develop knowledge, skills, values, and behaviors.

In developing economies, informal entrepreneurs face a myriad of challenges including poor knowledge of product and market, poor network and resource sharing. The entrepreneurship education approach is often applied to promote entrepreneurial awareness (based on learning-about entrepreneurship, learning-to-do and knowledge about business start-up) that helps to develop the competencies necessary to identify and act on opportunities. Achievement of entrepreneurial culture and competencies require a pedagogical shift in the mind-set of teachers to make their teaching more entrepreneurial (Costa, Santos, Wach, & Caetano, 2018; Eijdenberg, Isaga, Paas, & Masurel, 2021; Lackéus & Sävetun, 2019).

Entrepreneurial resources include tangible and intangibles resources such as human capital (know-how or tacit knowledge, skills, and labor quality), financial, buildings, machinery, etc. These are important factors that determined business sustainability (Sallah & Caesar, 2020). The low level of education is a key factor affecting the level of informality and when the level of education increases, the level of informality decreases (ILO, 2018). The argument is that because entrepreneurship education focuses on raising entrepreneurial awareness and mind-set, it requires the adoption of educational approaches focusing on cognition (Costa et al., 2018). Also, entrepreneurship education can increase the competencies and innovation required for the creation of growth-oriented ventures (Roundy, 2017).

Proposition 3: High-growth entrepreneurship and growth-oriented ventures depend on the entrepreneurship environment and the ecosystem resilience.

The political, economic, cultural, social, technological, and legal environment are key determinants of EE and ecosystem resilience. Entrepreneurship development and growth depend so much on external factors such as demand conditions, access to markets, access to information, access to infrastructure, access to finance, import and export conditions. These act as either facilitator or barriers (Amésquita et al., 2018). The role of government is critical for the development of EE. Although evidence on the impact of government incentives and policy intervention (e.g. grants or subsidy) is mixed, there is evidence that both forms of policy intervention can be effective if appropriately designed and tailored to context (European Commission, 2017).

Internal factors (such as level of capital, size of the firm, managerial competencies, entrepreneurial orientation, experience, skills and knowledge) is another key determinant of growth-oriented EE. Some studies compare the impact of the interactions between organizational capabilities and business strategic orientation on performance for micro and small business (Agyapong & Acquaah, 2021). Arguably, the institutional environment, entrepreneurship stakeholders and culture are the three critical exogenous variables that determine the EE within a region. Stakeholder of entrepreneurship refers to groups or actors that either affect or be affected by the business environment. Although there are many EE actors, components, and factors involved in the formation of an EE, most of these factors are locally based (OECD, 2014; Sheriff & Muffatto, 2015).

Isenberg (2011) maintains that every EE is unique as it develops under idiosyncratic circumstances. Hence, EE determines whether a formal or informal economy will dominate. Figure 2 represents a model of Productive and Unproductive EE developed from Isenberg (2010, 2011) six EE interdependent actors that include policy, finance, culture, supports, human capital and markets. Where EE are unfavorable and less resilient, unproductive entrepreneurship (informal economy) will emerge. In a productive environment, output and firm growth will be higher, while in the unproductive environment, the result will be low output and high prevalence of informal micro-enterprises.

The model of Productive and Unproductive EE reveals a set of interconnected forces which formally and informally coalesce to connect, mediate and determine the entrepreneurial performance within the local, national and regional environment. Government is an important EE actor and stakeholder. Government support increases the coherence of EE participants' intentions, behaviors, and outcomes (Friedman, 2011). The government ensures that the prevalent EE within their domain can respond and adapt to disturbances by introducing policies that enable businesses to access resources, experiment, research, innovate and adapt technology. Governments invest in infrastructures and provide subsidies to encourage production and demand. Ease of business registration, the removal of import and export barriers could spur informal entrepreneurs to transit to the formal sector. Also, the promotion of robust entrepreneurship education, university research and schemes such as apprenticeship education,

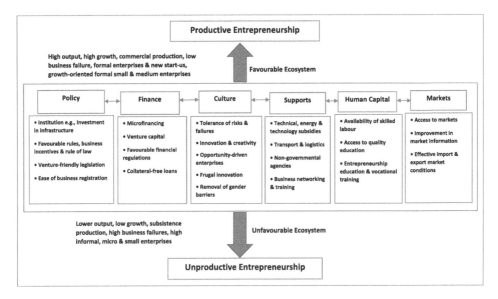

Figure 2. A model of productive and unproductive entrepreneurial ecosystem. Author's framework

employability education, career and counseling will be critical to the development of EE resilience.

Previous studies reveal that early-stage transition economies are typically characterized by ineffective formal institutions, which combine with weak or absent enforcement mechanisms (Welter & Smallbone, 2011). Although the impact of the institutional factor on entrepreneurship is mixed (positive and negative), it is generally agreed that conducive EE policies support necessary resources that promote innovations and productive start-ups (Mukiza & Kansheba, 2020; World Economic Forum, 2015). To start an entrepreneurial revolution, entrepreneurs and stakeholders must operate within some degree of common agenda to develop an EE environment that can be resilient against the market and non-market forces. A revolution of the informal economy will complement the government efforts in providing employment and making the national economy viable.

Discussion

This article examined the determinants of EE and ecosystem resilience that enable informal entrepreneurial revolution. An unproductive economy or high incidence of informality in all its forms has multiple adverse consequences to the local, national, and regional economies. On the positive assessment, the informal economy offers significant job creation and income generation potential, as well as the capacity to meet the needs of poor consumers by providing cheaper and more accessible goods and services (Bank of Industry [BOI], 2018). Also, the informal sector is crucial to the development of the urban economy. However, a high rate of informality has negative consequences such as tax evasion, lower wages, poor working conditions, lower productivity, and low economic growth.

African economies are dominated by the informal agricultural sector which produces 70% of the economy's total employment (United States Agency for International

Development [USAID], 2016). There is a significant difference in growth between firms in the formal sector and informal sector (Abdallah, 2017; Ghecham, 2010). Many African economies have recorded an increase in the growth of agriculture, manufacturing, consumer trade, construction, and other services. However, these sectors have maintained modest increases in productivity which have not supported job growth (USAID, 2016). More so, the growth is too low to lift the bottom half of the population out of poverty (World Bank, 2020). Besides, there is high level of corruption, high rate of crime, lack of access to capital, and poor state of infrastructure which stifle entrepreneurs who aspire to start a new business or grow their business (United States Agency for International Development [USAID], 2016). Although corruption helps to speed up decisions in developing countries, it deters entrepreneurs unwilling to engage in the practices, encourages illegal activities, black markets and loss of government revenues.

Arguably, the high rate of poverty in African is both a cause and a consequence of informality (ILO, 2018). However, it does not always translate that an informal entrepreneur would be better off as a formal entrepreneur (Maloney, 2004). The conditions of the EE have a greater impact on performance and productivity, regardless of the context (that is informal or formal economy). According to the report by McKinsey Global Institute (2014), African economic growth has been driven primarily by improving productivity. However, historical weaknesses in the agricultural sector and a poorly functioning urbanization process have prevented most citizens from benefiting from this growth (McKinsey Global Institute, 2014).

The outcome of the dominant informal ecosystem (Trading Economics, 2020) is that employment creation remains weak and insufficient to absorb the fast-growing labor force, resulting in a high rate of unemployment (World Bank, 2020). Although entrepreneurship education and awareness have become popular in many societies, the pedagogy of teaching and learning are weak to make significant changes (Igwe et al., 2019; Nwajiuba, Igwe, Akinsola-Obatolu, Icha-Ituma, & Binuomote, 2020b; Okolie, Igwe, Eneje, Nwosu, & Mlanga, 2019). Historically, interventions in the informal sector have been focused on how to regulate businesses, and effectively integrate them into the formal economy (Bank of Industry [BOI], 2018). As such, limited emphasis has been given to identifying the drivers of growth, building sustainable EE resilience and overcoming environmental challenges.

Conclusion and implications

The EE and ecosystem resilience determine the responses to the disruptions, changes, adaptions, and evolving of entrepreneurship over time. To start an informal entrepreneurial revolution, policymakers need to rethink policies, informal and formal regulations. The marginalization of the informal sector needs to change, and policies need to focus on how to improve the sector to make it more productive and resourceful. For instance, the provision of readily accessible microfinancing, small business training, educational apprenticeship and small-scale start-up funding will encourage entrepreneurs to develop business activities in the formal sector. Although there is consensus that creating conducive EE could be useful road maps for economic growth and poverty reduction in Africa (Sheriff & Muffatto, 2015), creating productive EE poses various challenges for policymakers (Mason & Brown, 2014).

EE typically represent the greatest challenge for economic growth. In this article, frugal, ecosystem resilience and EE assessments are based on an understanding of ecosystem landscape, the composition and configuration in response to disturbances, market and non-market forces. Policies aimed at institutional supports and investments are critical for the development of a favorable business environment. Some policies promote friendly EE such as simplifying business registration, export licensing procedures, favorable business taxation, access to finance, improvement in legal processes, access to market information, improvement of human capital competencies, entrepreneurship education and employability skills. However, many governments take a misguided approach toward developing favorable entrepreneurship policies (Friedman, 2011).

The model of Productive and Unproductive EE provide insights on how to start an informal entrepreneurial revolution to promote entrepreneurship and economic growth. Entrepreneurship has benefits to workers, firms, government and societies and is crucial for the achievement of sustainable development, inclusive development, reduction in inequality and poverty. It provides a foundation for innovation, effective resource allocation and value creation. In the light of the role of the informal sector in developing countries in meeting the economic dimension of sustainable development, there is a need for studies to focus on informal sector to understand and explore how to support and enable the sector.

It is important to note that a key challenge in many developing countries is the lack of interactions of the key actors of EE. In developing economies, some programmes have a positive effect and incremental results such as investment in agriculture, investment in information and communication technology (ICT), technological, green energy, road, railways, transport, high-quality education and health care. The integration of ecosystem resilience with the EE concept provides the basis for understanding how ecosystem structures interact to influence the types of entrepreneurial activities, disturbances, stressors and the capacity of the EE to support productive entrepreneurship or formal entrepreneurship.

Given the importance of the informal sector to employment and income generation to the poor and vulnerable population, we need to rethink the informal economy. Therefore, the EE concept offers both theoretical, practical and policy perspectives (Brown & Mason, 2017). These perspectives present opportunities to examine the state of entrepreneurship, EE actors and the role that governments play in the development of EE and ecosystem resilience. There is a need for more studies to focus on analyzing the EE, the environment, institutions, and prevailing culture. Future research should focus on the exploration of constraints most relevant to African countries and how to integrate frugal innovation with industrial and technological innovations to promote sustainable development and EE resilience.

Acknowledgement

This article has not been published or submitted elsewhere. We would like to thank the editors and reviewers for their recommendations that led to improvement of this manuscript.

Disclosure statement

No potential conflict of interest was reported by the author(s).

ORCID

Paul Agu Igwe http://orcid.org/0000-0003-3624-1861

References

Abdallah, G. K. (2017). Differences between firms from the formal sector and the informal sector in terms of growth: Empirical evidence from Tanzania. *Journal of Entrepreneurship in Emerging Economies, 9*(2), 121–143.

Acs, Z. J., Audretsch, D. B., Lehmann, E. E., & Licht, G. (2016). National systems of entrepreneurship. *Small Business Economics, 46*(4), 527–535.

African Development Bank. (2013, March 27). *Recognizing Africa's informal sector*. Retrieved from https://www.afdb.org/en/blogs/afdb-championing-inclusive-growth-across-africa/post/recognizing-africas-informal-sector-11645/

Agyapong, A., & Acquaah, M. (2021). Organizational capabilities, business strategic orientation, and performance in family and non-family businesses in a sub-Saharan African Economy. *Journal of African Business*, 1–29. doi:10.1080/15228916.2021.1907158

Ajekwu, C. C. (2017). Effect of culture on entrepreneurship in Nigeria. *International Journal of Business and Management Invention, 6*(2), 1–6.

Al-Mataani, R., Wainwright, T., & Demirel, P. (2017). Hidden entrepreneurs: Informal practices within the formal economy. *European Management Review, 14*(4), 361–376.

Amésquita, C. F., Morales, O., & Rees, G. H. (2018). Understanding the intentions of informal entrepreneurs in Peru. *Journal of Entrepreneurship in Emerging Economies, 10*(3), 489–510.

Anggadwita, G., Ramadani, V., & Ratten, V. (2017). Sociocultural environments and emerging economy entrepreneurship women entrepreneurs in Indonesia. *Journal of Entrepreneurship in Emerging Economies, 9*(1), 85–96.

Bank of Industry. (2018, May). *Economic development through the Nigerian Informal Sector: A BOI perspective* (Working Paper Series, 2). Retrieved from https://www.boi.ng/wp-content/uploads/2018/05/BOI-Working-Paper-Series-No2_Economic-Development-through-the-Nigerian-Informal-Sector-A-BOI-perspective.pdf

Beliaeva, T., Ferasso, M., Kraus, S., & Damke, E. (2020). Dynamics of digital entrepreneurship and the innovation ecosystem: A multilevel perspective. *International Journal of Entrepreneurial Behavior & Research, 26*(2), 266–284.

Block, J. H., Fisch, C. O., & van Praag, M. (2017). The Schumpeterian entrepreneur: A review of the empirical evidence on the antecedents, behaviour and consequences of innovative entrepreneurship. *Industry and Innovation, 24*(1), 61–95.

Brown, R., & Mason, C. (2017). Looking inside the spiky bits: A critical review and conceptualisation of entrepreneurial ecosystems. *Small Business Economics, 49*(1), 11–30.

Bruns, K., Bosma, N., Sanders, M., & Schramm, M. (2017). Searching for the existence of entrepreneurial ecosystems: A regional cross-section growth regression approach. *Small Business Economics, 49*(1), 31–35.

Chambers, J. C., Allen, C. R., & Cushman, S. A. (2019). Operationalizing ecological resilience concepts for managing species and ecosystems at risk. *Frontiers in Ecology and Evolution, 7*, 241–259.

Chen, G., & Hamori, S. (2009). *Formal employment, informal employment and income differentials in Urban China* (MPRA Paper, No. 17585). posted 30 Sep 2009 08:27 UTC. Retrieved from https://mpra.ub.uni-muenchen.de/17585/

Costa, S. F., Santos, S. C., Wach, D., & Caetano, A. (2018). Recognizing opportunities across campus: The effects of cognitive training and entrepreneurial passion on the business opportunity prototype. *Journal of Small Business Management, 56*(1), 51–75.

DiMaggio, P. J., & Powell, W. W. (1991). Introduction. In W. W. Powell & P. J. DiMaggio (Eds.), *The new institutionalism in organizational analysis*. Chicago: University of Chicago Press.

Eijdenberg, E. L., Isaga, N. M., Paas, L. J., & Masurel, E. (2021). Fluid entrepreneurial motivations in Tanzania. *Journal of African Business, 22*(2), 171–189.

Ekekwe, N. (2016, July 11). Why African entrepreneurship is booming? *Harvard Business Review*. Retrieved from https://hbr.org/2016/07/why-african-entrepreneurship-is-booming

European Commission. (2017). *Effectiveness of tax incentives for venture capital and business angels to foster the investment of SMEs and start-ups* (Final Report, TAXUD/2015/DE/330, FWC No. TAXUD/2015/CC/131). Retrieved from https://ec.europa.eu/taxation_customs/sites/taxation/files/taxation_paper_69_vc-ba.pdf

Ezeoha, A. E., & Icha-Ituma, A. (2017). Barriers to business development in Nigeria. In A. Akinyoade, T. Dietz, & C. Uche (Eds.), *Entrepreneurship in Africa series: African dynamics* (p. 15). Netherlands: BRILL.

Falk, D. A., Watts, A. C., & Thode, A. E. (2019). Scaling ecological resilience. *Frontiers in Ecology and Evolution, 7*, 275–292.

Feldman, M., & Lowe, N. (2017). Evidence-based economic development policy. *Innovations, 11*(3/4), 1–18.

Fishman, A., Don-Yehiya, H., & Schreiber, A. (2018). Too big to succeed or too big to fail? *Small Business Economics, 51*(4), 811–822.

Freire-Gibb, L. C., & Nielsen, K. (2014). Entrepreneurship within urban and rural areas: Creative people and social networks. *Regional Studies, 48*(1), 139–153.

Friedman, B. A. (2011). The relationship between governance effectiveness and entrepreneurship". *International Journal of Humanities and Social Science, 1*(17), 221–235.

GEM. (2015). *Africa's young entrepreneurs: Unlocking the Potential for a better future.* Retrieved May 06, 2018, from https://www.idrc.ca/sites/default/files/sp/Documents%20EN/Africas-Young-Entrepreneurs-Unlocking-the-Potential-for-a-Brighter-Future.pdf

GEM. (2016/2017). *Global report.* Retrieved from https://www.babson.edu/Academics/centers/blank-center/global-research/gem/Documents/GEM%202016-2017%20Global%20Report.pdf

GEM. (2018). *Global report.* Retrieved from file:///C:/Users/SurfBook/Downloads/rev-gem-2017-2018-global-report-revised-1527266790-1548584425-1549359513.pdf

Ghecham, M. A. (2010). How the interaction between formal and informal institutional constraints determines the investment growth of firms in Egypt. *Journal of African Business, 11*(2), 163–181.

Global Entrepreneurship Monitor. (2014). *Africa's young entrepreneurs: Unlocking the potential for a better future.* UK: Global Entrepreneurship Monitor. Retrieved November 25, 2017, from file:///H:/Downloads/1425737316GEM_UK_2014_final.pdf

Guma, P. K. (2015). Business in the urban informal economy: Barriers to women's entrepreneurship in Uganda. *Journal of African Business, 16*(3), 305–321.

Igwe, P. A. (2020). Determinants of household income and employment choices in the rural agripreneurship economy. *Studies in Agricultural Economics, 122*(2), 96–103.

Igwe, P. A., Amaugo, A. N., Ogundana, O. M., Egere, O. M., & Anigbo, J. A. (2018). Factors affecting the investment climate, SMEs productivity and entrepreneurship in Nigeria. *European Journal of Sustainable Development, 7*(1), 182–200.

Igwe, P. A., Hack-polay, D., Mendy, J., Fuller, T., & Lock, D. (2019). Improving higher education standards through reengineering in West African Universities - A case study of Nigeria. *Studies in Higher Education*, 1–14. doi:10.1080/03075079.2019.1698534

Igwe, P. A., Lock, D., & Rugara, D. G. (2020). What factors determine the development of employability skills in Nigerian higher education? *Innovations in Education and Teaching International*, 1–12. doi:10.1080/14703297.2020.1850319

Igwe, P. A., Madichie, N. O., & Newbery, R. (2019). Determinants of livelihood choices and artisanal entrepreneurship in Nigeria. *International Journal of Entrepreneurial Behavior & Research, 25*(4), 674–697.

Igwe, P. A., Ochinanwata, C., & Madichie, N. O. (2021). The 'Isms' of regional integration: What do underlying interstate preferences hold for the ECOWAS Union? *Politics & Policy, 49*(2), 280–308.

Igwe, P. A., Odunukan, K., Rahman, M., Rugara, D. G., & Ochinanwata, C. (2020). How entrepreneurship ecosystem influences the development of frugal innovation and informal entrepreneurship? *Thunderbird International Business Review, 62*(5), 475–488.

Igwe, P. A., Okolie, U. C., & Nwokoro, C. V. (2021). Towards a responsible entrepreneurship education and the future of the workforce. *The International Journal of Management Education, 19*(1), 100300.

ILO. (2014). *Transitioning from the informal to the formal economy*. International Labour Conference 103rd Session 2014, Report, *V*(1), International Labour Office, Geneva.

ILO. (2018). *Informal economy*. Retrieved from https://www.ilo.org/global/about-the-ilo/news room/news/WCMS_627189/lang–en/index.htm

International Labour Organization. (1993, January). *Resolutions concerning statistics of employment in the informal sector*. Adopted by the 15th International Conference of Labour Statisticians, para. 5, Geneva. Retrieved from https://stats.oecd.org/glossary/detail.asp?ID=1350

International Monetary Fund. (2017, July 10). *The informal economy in Sub-Saharan Africa: Size and determinants* (Working Paper No. 17/156). Retrieved from https://www.imf.org/en/Publications/WP/Issues/2017/07/10/The-Informal-Economy-in-Sub-Saharan-Africa-Size-and-Determinants-45017

Isenberg, D. (2014). What an entrepreneurship ecosystem actually is? *Harvard Business Review*, [Online]. Retrieved from https://hbr.org/2014/05/what-an-entrepreneurial-ecosystem-actually-is

Isenberg, D. J. (2010). How to start an entrepreneurial revolution. *Harvard Business Review, 88*(6), 40–50.

Isenberg, D. J. (2011). *The entrepreneurship ecosystem strategy as a new paradigm for economic policy: Principles for cultivating entrepreneurship*. Paper presented at the Institute of International and European Affairs, Dublin.

Kellermanns, F., Walter, J., Crook, T. R., Kemmerer, B., & Narayanan, V. (2016). The resource-based view in entrepreneurship: A content-analytical comparison of researchers' and entrepreneurs' views. *Journal of Small Business Management, 54*(1), 26–48.

Kim, Y., & Loayza, N. V. (2017). *Productivity and its determinants: Innovation, education, efficiency, infrastructure, and institutions*. The World Bank. Retrieved from http://pubdocs.worldbank.org/en/378031511165998244/Productivity-and-its-determinants-25-October-2017.pdf

Kuckertz, A. (2019). Let's take the entrepreneurial ecosystem metaphor seriously". *Journal of Business Venturing Insights, 11*, 1–24.

Lackéus, M., & Sävetun, C. (2019). Assessing the impact of enterprise education in three leading Swedish compulsory schools. *Journal of Small Business Management, 57*(sup1), 33–59.

Levin, S. (2015). *Ecological resilience*. Encyclopedia Britannica. Retrieved from https://www.britannica.com/science/ecological-resilience

Mack, E., & Mayer, H. (2015). The evolutionary dynamics of entrepreneurial ecosystems. *Urban Studies, 53*(10), 2118–2133.

Madichie, N. O. (2009). Breaking the glass ceiling in Nigeria: A review of women's entrepreneurship. *Journal of African Business, 10*(1), 51–66.

Madichie, N. O., Hinson, R. E., & Ibrahim, M. (2013). A reconceptualization of entrepreneurial orientation in an emerging market insurance company. *Journal of African Business, 14*(3), 202–214.

Madichie, N. O., Nkamnebe, A. D., & Idemobi, E. I. (2008). Cultural determinants of entrepreneurial emergence in a typical sub-Sahara African context. *Journal of Enterprising Communities: People and Places in the Global Economy, 2*(4), 285–299.

Mahoney, J. T., & Michael, S. C. (2005). *Resources, capabilities and entrepreneurial perceptions* (working paper). The University of Illinois at Urbana–Champaign Retrieved from https://pdfs.semanticscholar.org/7af1/71ddab9b9fc5e6fa6b920cce6c6d553be441.pdf

Maloney, W. F. (2004). Informality revisited. *World Development, 32*(7), 1159–1178.

Maloney, W.F. (1999). Does informality imply segmentation in urban labor markets? Evidence from sectoral transitions in Mexico. *World Bank Economic Review,13*(2): 275–302.

Maroufkhani, P., Wagner, R., Khairuzzaman, W., & Ismail, W. (2018). Entrepreneurial ecosystems: A systematic review. *Journal of Enterprising Communities: People and Places in the Global Economy, 12*(4), 545–564.

Mason, C., & Brown, R. (2014). *Entrepreneurial ecosystems and growth-oriented entrepreneurship.* Background paper prepared for the workshop organised by the OECD LEED Programme and the Dutch Ministry of Economic Affairs, The Hague, Netherlands, 7th November 2013. Final Version: January 2014. Retrieved from https://www.oecd.org/cfe/leed/entrepreneurial-ecosystems.pdf

Mathias, B. D., Solomon, S. J., & Madison, K. (2017). After the harvest: A stewardship perspective on entrepreneurship and philanthropy. *Journal of Business Venturing, 32*(4), 385–404.

McGowan, P., Cooper, S., Durkin, M., & O'Kane, C. (2015). The influence of social and human capital in developing young women as entrepreneurial business leaders. *Journal of Small Business Management, 53*(3), 645–661.

McKinsey Global Institute. (2014). *Nigeria's renewal: Delivering inclusive growth in Africa's largest economy.* Retrieved from https://www.mckinsey.com/~/media/mckinsey/featured%20insights/Middle%20East%20and%20Africa/Nigerias%20renewal%20Delivering%20inclusive%20growth/MGI_Nigerias_renewal_Full_report.ashx

Meagher, K. (2018). Cannibalizing the informal economy: Frugal innovation and economic inclusion in Africa". *The European Journal of Development Research, 30*(2), 17–33.

Mukiza, J., & Kansheba, P. (2020). Small business and entrepreneurship in Africa: The nexus of entrepreneurial ecosystems and productive entrepreneurship. *Small Enterprise Research, 27*(2), 110–124.

Mwobobia, F. (2012). The challenges facing small-scale women entrepreneurs: A case of Kenya. *International Journal of Business Administration, 3*, 112–121.

Naudé, W. (2010). Entrepreneurship, developing countries, and development economics: New approaches and insights. *Small Business Economics, 34*(1), 1–12.

North, D. C. (1990). *Institutions, institutional change, and economic performance.* Cambridge, UK: Cambridge University Press.

Nwajiuba, C. A., Igwe, P. A., Akinsola-Obatolu, A. D., Icha-Ituma, A., & Binuomote, M. O. (2020b). What can be done to improve higher education quality and graduate employability? A Stakeholder approach. *Industry and Higher Education, 34*(5), 358–367.

Nwajiuba, C. A., Igwe, P. A., Binuomote, M. O., Nwajiuba, A. O., & Nwekpa, K. C. (2020a). The barriers to high-growth enterprises: What do businesses in Africa experience? *European Journal of Sustainable Development, 9*(1), 1–18.

OECD. (2014). *Entrepreneurial ecosystems and growth-oriented entrepreneurship.* Paris: Author. Retrieved from http://www.oecd.org/cfe/leed/entrepreneurial-ecosystems.pdf

OECD. (2017). *Entrepreneurship at a Glance 2017.* Paris: Author. Retrieved from http://dx.doi.org/10.1787/entrepreneur_aag-2017-en

OECD. (2019). *Tackling vulnerability in the informal economy* (pp. 155–165). Author. Retrieved from https://www.oecd-ilibrary.org/development/tackling-vulnerability-in-the-informal-economy_103bf23e-en

Okolie, U. C., Ehiobuche, C., Igwe, P. A., Agha-Okoro, M. A., & Onwe, C. C. (2021). Women entrepreneurship and poverty alleviation: Understanding the economic and socio-cultural context of the Igbo Women's basket weaving enterprise in Nigeria. *Journal of African Business*, 1–20. doi:10.1080/15228916.2021.1874781

Okolie, U. C., Igwe, P. A., Ayoola, A. A., Nwosu, H. E., Kanu, C., & Mong, I. K. (2021, March). Entrepreneurial competencies of undergraduate students: The case of universities in Nigeria. *The International Journal of Management Education, 19*(1), 100452.

Okolie, U. C., Igwe, P. A., Eneje, B. C., Nwosu, H., & Mlanga, S. (2019). Enhancing graduate employability: Why do higher education institutions have problems with teaching generic skills? *Policy Futures in Education, 18*(2), 294–313.

Olomi, D., Charles, G., & Juma, N. (2018). An inclusive approach to regulating the second economy: A tale of four Sub-Saharan African economies. *Journal of Entrepreneurship in Emerging Economies, 10*(3), 447–471.

Özkundakci, D., & Lehmann, M. K. (2019). Lake resilience: Concept, observation and management. *New Zealand Journal of Marine and Freshwater Research*, 53(4), 481–488.

Pereira, R., Ribeiro, M. C., Manuel, O., Marques, M., Rua, L., & Martins, D. (2019). *Is there entrepreneurship within the public sector? A literature review*. Handbook of Entrepreneurial Orientation and Opportunities for Global Economic Growth. Chapter 005, IGI Global. Retrieved from https://www.irma-international.org/chapter/is-there-entrepreneurship-within-the-public-sector/216639/

Prabhu, J. (2017). Frugal innovation: Doing more with less for more. *Philosophical Transactions of the Royal Society A*, 375(2095), 2016037220160372.

Pradhan, M., & van Soest, A. (1997). Household Labor supply in urban areas of Bolivia. *Review of Economics and Statistics*, 79(2), 300–310.

Ram, M., Edwards, P., Jones, T., & Villares-Varela, M. (2017). From the informal economy to the meaning of informality: Developing theory on firms and their workers. *International Journal of Sociology and Social Policy*, 37(7/8), 361–373.

Ratten, V., & Jones, P. (2018). Bringing Africa into entrepreneurship research. In L.-P. Dana, B. Q. Honyenuga, & V. Ratten (Eds.), *Challenges and opportunities for doing business, Palgrave studies of entrepreneurship in Africa*. Cheltenham: Palgrave Macmillan.

Roundy, P. T. (2017). Social entrepreneurship and entrepreneurial ecosystems: Complementary or disjoint phenomena? *International Journal of Social Economics*, 44(9), 1252–1267.

Roundy, P. T., Brockman, B. K., & Bradshaw, M. (2017). The resilience of entrepreneurial ecosystems. *Journal of Business Venturing Insights*, 8(2017), 99–104.

Rwelamila, P. D., & Ssegawa, J. K. (2014). The African project failure syndrome: The conundrum of project management knowledge base - The case of SADC. *Journal of African Business*, 15(3), 211–224.

Sallah, C. A., & Caesar, L. D. (2020). Intangible resources and the growth of women businesses: Empirical evidence from an emerging market economy. *Journal of Entrepreneurship in Emerging Economies*, 12(3), 329–355.

Saúde, S., Hermozilha, P., & Borrero, J. D. (2020). *The influence of the local ecosystem on entrepreneurial intentions: A study with entrepreneurs and potential entrepreneurs of Beja (Portugal) and Huelva (Spain)*. Handbook of Research on Approaches to Alternative Entrepreneurship Opportunities. Chapter 006. IGI Global. doi:10.4018/978-1-7998-1981-3

Seo, M., & Creed, W. E. D. (2002). Institutional contradictions, praxis, and institutional change: A dialectical perspective. *Academy of Management Review*, 27(2), 222–247.

Sheriff, M., & Muffatto, M. (2015). The present state of entrepreneurship ecosystems in selected countries in Africa. *African Journal of Economic and Management Studies*, 6(1), 17–54.

Shwetzer, C., Maritz, A., & Nguyen, Q. (2019). Entrepreneurial ecosystems: A holistic and dynamic approach. *Journal of Industry-University Collaboration*, 1(2), 79–95.

Stam, E., & Van De Ven, A. (2019). Entrepreneurial ecosystem elements. *Small Business Economics*, 56(2), 809–832.

Sutter, C., Webb, J., Kistruck, G., Ketchen, D. J., & Ireland, R. D. (2017). Transitioning entrepreneurs from informal to formal markets. *Journal of Business Venturing*, 32(4), 420–442.

Thornton, P. H., Ocasio, W., & Lounsbury, M. (2012). *The institutional logics perspective*. Oxford, UK: Wiley Online Library.

Thoughtwork. (2014). *Frugal innovation in Africa*. Retrieved from https://www.thoughtworks.com/insights/blog/frugal-innovation-africa-interview

Trading Economics. (2020). *Nigerian unemployment rate*. Retrieved from https://tradingeconomics.com/nigeria/unemployment-rate

United States Agency for International Development. (2016). *Workforce development & youth employment in Nigeria* (AID Contract # AID-OAA-I-15-00034/AID-OAA-TO-15-00011). Retrieved from https://www.youthpower.org/sites/default/files/Workforce%20Development%20and%20Youth%20Employment%20in%20Nigeria%20Desk%20Review%20Final%20Draft-Public%20Version%20(4).pdf

Vershinina, N., Beta, W. K., & Murithi, W. (2018). How does national culture enable or constrain entrepreneurship? Exploring the role of Harambee in Kenya. *Journal of Small Business and Enterprise Development, 25*(4), 687–704.

Welter, F., & Smallbone, D. (2011). Institutional perspectives on entrepreneurial behavior in challenging environments. *Journal of Small Business Management, 49*(1), 107–125.

Williams, N., & Vorley, T. (2015). The impact of institutional change on entrepreneurship in a crisis-hit economy: The case of Greece. *Entrepreneurship & Regional Development, 27*(1–2), 28–49.

World Bank. (2013). *Gender and transport*. Washington, DC: Author. Retrieved December 17, 2017, from http://www.worldbank.org/en/news/press-release/2013/09/24/societies-dismantle-gender-discrimination-world-bank-group-president-jim-yong-kim

World Bank. (2014). *Latin American entrepreneurs: Many firms but little innovation*. Washington, DC: International Bank for Reconstruction and Development/The World Bank. Retrieved from http://www.worldbank.org/content/dam/Worldbank/document/LAC/LatinAmericanEntrepreneurs.pdf

World Bank. (2015, October 27). *Fact sheet: Doing business 2016 in Sub-Saharan Africa*. Retrieved March 9, 2017, from http://www.worldbank.org/en/region/afr/brief/fact-sheet-doing-business-2016-in-sub-saharan-africa.

World Bank. (2016, January). *Informal enterprises in Kenya*. Washington, DC, USA: Author.

World Bank. (2020). *World development report*. Retrieved from https://www.worldbank.org/en/publication/wdr2020

World Economic Forum. (2015). *Why we need to rethink the informal economy*. Retrieved from https://www.weforum.org/agenda/2015/06/why-we-need-to-rethink-the-informal-economy/

World Economic Forum. (2019). *World Economic Forum (2019). Three things Nigeria must do to end extreme poverty*. Retrieved from https://www.weforum.org/agenda/2019/03/90-million-nigerians-live-in-extreme-poverty-here-are-3-ways-to-bring-them-out/#:~:text=About%2090%20million%20people%20%2D%20roughly,the%20bottom%20of%20the%20table

The Effect of Militancy on Local and Informal Enterprises in Developing Countries: Evidence from Niger Delta

Ignatius Ekanem, Terence Jackson and Ayebaniminyo Munasuonyo

ABSTRACT

Militancy is a continuing process in many developing regions where entrepreneurial activities in the informal economy have the potential to transform lives leading to sustainable development through local initiatives. Often militancy originates in protest against global encroachment and defending the livelihoods of local communities. Yet this leads to detrimental effects on such initiatives. The study focuses on small and medium-sized enterprises (SMEs) in the Niger Delta in Nigeria and looks at how the lessons learned may be used in other developing regions facing similar issues. Findings suggest how violent conflict resulting in an adverse impact on enterprise development can be mediated by collective actions.

1. Introduction

Militancy is the use of confrontation method or violence to support a cause. It is an organized and sustained use of physical force that results in injury or death to individuals or damage to property (Getz & Oetzel, 2010). Militancy is different from military action as it is often non-governmental, while military action can be government-sponsored. Militancy, such as the type of the Niger Delta, arises as a result of the marginalization of the people, environmental degradation, corruption, injustice, and the divide and rule policy of the oil companies (Nwogwugwu, Alao, & Egwuonwu, 2012).

The aim of this study is specifically to explore the effect of militancy on small and medium enterprise development in the Niger Delta region of Nigeria and to discuss survival strategies for these businesses in the region. There has been a little study about the effects of militancy on enterprises or small business development in developing countries. Most of the research efforts in developing countries, and in the Niger Delta, in particular, have been focused on the causes of the conflicts, and multinational responses as well as the role of the state in conflict resolution.

In both developed and developing economies, the small and medium-sized enterprises (SMEs) sector is known to contribute significantly to economic growth and development (BIS, 2013; Ihua, 2009). This contribution includes job creation, wealth creation, and provision of products and services, as well as enhancing standards of living (Anyadike-Daness, Hart, & Du, 2013; Ihua, 2010).

Research studies, such as Grant (2003), have associated the pace of SME development with entrepreneurial environments which include the willingness of individuals to engage in entrepreneurial activities and business start-ups. Therefore, a peaceful business environment is a critical factor in SME development (Rettberg, Leiteritz, & Nasi, 2010), while a violent one can lead to high operating costs and reduction in operations and profit margins of companies generally.

The structure of this article commences with a theoretical framework developed from the literature on SME development and violent conflict in the developing world and in the Niger Delta in particular. We use the resource-based theory and social behavior theory within the entrepreneurial literature to make our conceptual case, which we discuss in the context of Rettberg's (2008) theory of costs of conflict. The methodological approach and research methods are discussed and the findings are presented from our empirical research based on interviews with owners and militants, and implications are discussed.

2. Entrepreneurial theory and costs of conflict

Resource-based theories focus on the way individual leverage different types of resources to get entrepreneurial efforts off the ground (Barney, 1991). Access to capital improves the chances of getting a new venture off the ground, but entrepreneurs often start ventures, especially in the informal economy, with little ready capital (Newbert, 2007). Other types of resource entrepreneurs might leverage include social networks and the information they provide, as well as human resources, including such attributes as the level of education and training. In some cases, the intangible elements of leadership the entrepreneur add to the mix operate as resources that a business cannot replace (Newbert, 2007). Hence, not only could we surmise that some resources in the Delta region and other developing regions may be limited or at least restricted, such as start-up capital, other intrinsic resources, such as skills and experience may also be in short supply. This may put SMEs in a vulnerable position. The effects of violent conflict can only exacerbate this vulnerability.

Reynolds (1991) focuses on the social contexts that relate to entrepreneurial opportunity. Although social networks are seen as a resource in resource-based theory, in Reynolds (1991) social behavior theory the focus is on building social relationships and bonds that promote trust and not opportunism: the entrepreneur should not take undue advantage of people to be successful. Success comes as a result of keeping faith in the people. The resource-based theory is instrumental in that social networks are seen to be there as a resource to be used, rather than being part of the social fabric within which entrepreneurs operate as part of the community within which and of which they serve. This view is supported in the indigenous entrepreneurship literature that suggests that the collective nature of indigenous societies is often based on kinship, forming the basis of governance and decision-making structures, as well as the social and economic structures of production, distribution, and consumption (Peredo & McLean, 2010).

These approaches place entrepreneurship within the context of culture and examine how cultural forces, such as social attitudes, shape both the perception of entrepreneurship and the behaviors of entrepreneurs. Thus, cultural environments can produce attitude differences (Baskerville, 2003) as well as entrepreneurial behavior differences (Shane,

1994). For example, the literature on indigenous entrepreneurship suggests that trading and entrepreneurship are often based not on market needs, but on kinship ties (Dana, 2015), where forms of exchange are based on social purposes. Although the individual profit motive may exist, it is subordinated to meeting community needs and objectives. Referring to communities in central America Berkes. and Adhikari. (2006, p. 11) suggest that 'The social role of many of these enterprises is apparent in terms of providing local employment, making use of talents and resources locally available, and sharing profits among community members.' Dana (2015) cites other studies in South Africa, Hawaii, and the Andes that suggest that the emphasis in these communities is not on wealth creation, but where economic goals are channeled toward social and community ends.

Such theories predominantly have been crafted with no reference to conflict zones. A key contribution to understanding the influence of conflict on private business enterprises has been made by Rettberg (2008) in her study in Colombia. She identifies eleven direct and indirect costs of conflict. These are direct costs including extortion payments, threats, direct attacks on the company or employees, decreases in sales as a result of shutdowns; and indirect costs including loss of business opportunities, delays in delivery of goods, increases in security and insurance expenses, changes in demand and in the market, disruptions of the distribution and transport networks, opportunity costs, and taxes.

One of Rettberg's (2008) main conclusions from her survey was that the costs of the conflict have impeded economic activity, and the costs have not been evenly spread (Rettberg, 2013). For instance, factors, such as company size, sector of the economy, and location, have determined how the conflict has affected companies. According to the survey, the majority of Colombian businesses have suffered from indirect costs (for example, loss of business opportunities, delays in merchandize distribution, opportunity costs, investments in security and insurance, and taxes) rather than direct costs (for example, kidnappings, extortion, and attacks against staff and/or operations). Similar indirect costs were identified as a result of the conflict in Southern Sudan (Abdelnour et al., 2008).

Rettberg (2013) also argues that larger companies were more likely to report costs than smaller ones. Businesses with nationwide operations were more likely to make extortion payments to illegal armed groups and experience logistical disruptions than were companies with regional or local operations. These findings by Rettberg (2013) and Abdelnour et al. (2008) provide a better understanding of the kinds of impacts the Colombian and Sudan armed conflicts have had on economic activity, as well as the types of enterprises and sectors that are most vulnerable (or less exposed and more resilient) to certain costs associated with the conflict. The results also indicate links between armed conflict and costs to SMEs.

The Niger Delta is an important area for oil production and a key component in both Nigeria's development and environmental degradation. The latter, and associated militant action in the region, has brought it into the public eye. Yet there is a lack of knowledge in this region of the costs of conflict on local enterprises which this study aims to fill.

3. Firms' response to conflict

Oetzel and Getz (2012) provide the framework for firms' response to the crisis. Oetzel and Getz (2012) suggest that non-business actors such as policy-makers and non-governmental organizations (NGOs) expect private businesses to participate in conflict resolution activities. However, the role of businesses and entrepreneurial practices in restoring peace is currently underexplored (Abdelnour & Branzei, 2009; Oetzel, Westermann-Behalo, Koerber, Fort, & Rivera, 2010).

Research evidence indicates that firms are increasingly taking responsibility to respond to the crisis in their countries of operation (Kolt & Lenfant, 2010). By the same token, Branzei and Abdelnour (2010) argue that firms are able to reduce the risks from the crisis, survive and obtain competitive advantage from responding effectively to adverse conditions and crisis. For example, Oetzel and Getz (2012) suggest that small firms respond to crisis indirectly to mitigate the effect of the crisis by adopting supplementary activities aimed at minimizing tensions in the society.

Some tactics identified in the literature that may help businesses to deal with crisis include business support to small businesses in the form of microfinance, skills training, enterprise/market activity (Abdelnour et al., 2008), withholding payments, or refraining from selling to those who facilitate the crisis (Collier, 2007). The response may include engaging in philanthropic activities to help victims of the crisis (Luo, 2006). It may also include supporting educational programs and implementing training programs aimed at reducing the impact of crisis within the enterprises (Jamali & Mirshak, 2010; Kolt & Lenfant, 2010).

Businesses may respond to conflicts either by acting alone or with other organizations (Oetzel & Getz, 2012). These organizations may include other private sector organizations, non-governmental organizations (NGOs), and even inter-governmental organizations or agencies of the local government. The patterns of response may be different according to the types of business and geographical location of the crisis (Dai, Eden, & Beamish, 2013; Kolt & Lenfant, 2010). Getz and Oetzel (2010) argue that responding to crisis may help businesses to reduce the rate of employee turnover and avoid loss of assets. It also helps to prevent interruption of cash-flows and improve relations with the community.

By the same token, it can be argued that it might not be advantageous to the businesses to seek crisis resolutions because this might attract more competitors to relocate to the Niger Delta which may be perceived as wealthy (having an economy largely based on oil revenues). People are spontaneously attracted to the oil industry, often abandoning their original activity because the oil industry is economically and socially attractive (Renouard & Lado, 2012).

4. Investigating SMEs and conflict in the Niger Delta

The empirical study aimed to investigate how militancy affects local and informal enterprises and how business owners respond to conflict, in relation to theories of entrepreneurial development and conflict. It was important to obtain the perceptions of both SME owners/managers as well as militant leaders through in-depth interviews as well as direct observation (Crawford, Dimov, & McKelvey, 2016).

In this study, direct observation involved watching, listening and learning because not all the information is produced by informants responding to questions: they may be unsolicited (Ekanem, 2007). It provided the opportunity to observe some relevant behavior, and such observations served as yet another source of evidence in the case study (Yin, 2014). It also allowed access not only to what owner-managers said during the interview but also how they said it through symbolic language, including body language. The non-verbal language was found to be of equal importance as real feelings were constantly communicated, in addition to verbal language, in the language of behavior. The non-verbal language was noted down in writing during observation by the interviewer and helped in the interpretation of the data collected. This method, amongst other benefits, enabled the aims of the research to be more effectively achieved. It also enhanced the richness and depth of the data collected despite the relatively small sample size.

The case study firms consisted of eight small companies; four were from the oil sector while the other four were from the non-oil sector. The firms were located in the three core states of the Niger Delta region as indicated in Table 1. Three militant leaders were interviewed for the study. Interviews with the business owners lasted for one and half hours, while those with the militant leaders lasted for 45 min. An Enterprise Agency executive was also interviewed as a key informant and the interview lasted for about an hour. The Enterprise Agency executive also acted as a 'gatekeeper' introducing the interviewer (the third author) to small businesses in the area.

The participants were drawn from two sectors, namely, the oil sector and the non-oil sector. The businesses in the oil sector included, marine transport, supplies and logistics, and oil products marketing, while those in the non-oil sector included a hairdressing salon, trading/merchandising, communication, and general contracts. Participants were purposively selected through the help of the gatekeeper. Snowball sampling technique, where interviewed businesses recommended other businesses among their acquaintances, was also used in line with Robson's (2002) argument that snowball sampling is useful when there is difficulty in identifying members of the population. The selection criteria specified that the firms had to consist of those with less than 100 employees, which were based in the core Niger Delta region of Bayelsa, Delta, and River states. The firms also had to be in existence for at least a year, independently owned, and of different ages and sizes to be included in the sample.

The interviews were divided into three parts. The first part of the interview was designed to explore the initial boundaries for the research as well as to provide details of the SME's background. This section, gathering general information about the organization, was not conducted with the militant leaders because of obvious safety or security issues. This section also focused on the profile and nature of business of the SMEs, turnover, and the number of paid employees. This exploratory part of the interview helped to reveal the major issues of the research as well as building rapport with the interviewees (Ekanem, 2007).

The second and the third sections of the interview were designed to understand the interviewees' general feelings about the Niger Delta struggle as well as their experiences and understanding of militants' activities. These helped to reveal their frame of reference when responding to the main issues, such as influences of militants' actions and ways of dealing with the challenge of militancy.

Table 1 Company Profiles and Results.

1 Company	2 Sector	3 Age (Yrs. in Bus.)	4 No. of employees	5 Turnover	6 Location	7 Effect of militancy	8 Conflict costs	9 Collective actions for dealing with challenges
Oil Sector SMEs								
1	Marine transport	15	20	£2 m	Yenagoa, Bayelsa	Greatest impediment to SME development; making demand for resource control through hijacking/kidnapping, bunkering and vandalism; doing business in the area is not worthwhile; extortion payments; threats; corruption; closures; no roads, water and electricity.	Direct attacks on the company/employees; Threats; Extortion payments; Decreases in sales as a result of temporary or longer-term shut downs; Changes in demand and in the market; Disruptions of the distribution and transport networks; Loss business opportunities	Providing financial help and mentoring initiatives
2	Catering services	20	22	£500k	Brass, Bayelsa	Closure of business units, losses as well as folding-up of enterprises; no security for businesses in the region; lack of infrastructure.	Decreases in sales as a result of temporary or longer-term shut downs; Increases in security and insurance expenses	Philanthropic activities Refusing to sell to militants Condemning violence/ continuing business as normal
3	Supplies and logistics	10	7	£800k	Warri, Delta State	All enterprises and others struggle as a result of militancy; greatest fear about doing business in the region is security; closures; loss of land and compensation.	Decreases in sales as a result of temporary or longer-term shut downs; Loss business opportunities.	Supporting small business development Refusing to sell to militants Condemning violence/ continuing business as normal

(*Continued*)

Table 1 (Continued).

1 Company	2 Sector	3 Age (Yrs. in Bus.)	4 No. of employees	5 Turnover	6 Location	7 Effect of militancy	8 Conflict costs	9 Collective actions for dealing with challenges
4	Oil products marketing distribution and transport networks.	8	20	£3 m	Port Harcourt, Rivers State		Seeking control through demands for money, corruption; threats, bunkering, vandalism and blackmails. Supporting small business development	Extortion payments; Threats; Direct attacks on the company/ employees; Disruptions of the Non-oil Sector SMEs
5	Hairdressing salon	9	12	£15k	Port Harcourt, Rivers State	Extortion payments and threats both in upland and riverine areas; loss of business opportunities; violence against market women, petty traders, fast food sellers and other small businesses; lack of capital.	Direct attacks on the company/employees; Threats; Decreases in sales as a result of temporary or longer-term shut downs; Loss business opportunities; Opportunity costs.	Supporting small business development
6	Trading/ merchandising	22	60	£25k	Sapele, Delta State	It constitutes a serious impediment to growth of businesses; lack of infrastructure; closure of businesses; lack of finance and business opportunities.	Decreases in sales as a result of temporary or longer-term shut downs; Loss business opportunities; Direct attacks on the company/ employees	Supporting small business development Condemning violence/ continuing business as normal

(Continued)

Table 1 (Continued).

1 Company	2 Sector	3 Age (Yrs. in Bus.)	4 No. of employees	5 Turnover	6 Location	7 Effect of militancy	8 Conflict costs	9 Collective actions for dealing with challenges
7	Communications	9	15	£300k	Port Harcourt, Rivers State	Providing financial support and mentoring initiatives opportunities Refusing to sell to militants	Evil vices including rape; extortion against companies, corruption; prevents people doing legitimate businesses in the region.	Direct attacks on the company/ employees; Extortion payments; Loss business
8	General contracts	7	55	£1 m	Bonny, Rivers State	Extortion payments, threats and corruption on the oil and gas sector; it's not worthwhile to come here to do business; closures; lack of start-up finance; no roads, water and electricity.	Direct attacks on the company/employees; Threats; Loss business opportunities; Increases in security and insurance expenses; Decreases in sales as a result of temporary or longer-term shut downs.	Providing microcredit and mentoring initiatives Philanthropic activities

Consequently, the last segment focused in greater detail on the impact of militants' actions on local enterprises and ways of coping with the challenge. The militant leaders and enterprise agency executive were also interviewed as key informants, to gain further perspectives and check for the conflicting evidence.

The interviews were allowed to flow as a conversation around the influence of militants' activities and strategies for SME growth and development in the Niger Delta. Respondents were allowed freedom in their response and were encouraged to elaborate on their comments by probing gently. The aim was to give the interviewees a good deal of leeway to talk in their own terms (Ekanem, 2007; Spence & Rutherford, 2001). All interviews were recorded with the permission of the interviewees knowing that materials would be treated confidentially: an exciting experience as interviewees really opened up to talk freely.

5. Analyzing the data

Informed by grounded theory (Corbin & Strauss, 2008) the qualitative data were collected and analyzed using an inductive process of recording, tabulation, coding, and constantly comparing emerging codes and categories with data until meaningful ideas emerged (Fischer & Reuber, 2011; Yin, 2014). Categories were allowed to emerge according to the topics emphasized by each participant relating to militancy and its impact on their business. The process of analyzing the data began as soon as the researcher started collecting data. It was ongoing and inductive as the researcher was trying to make sense of the data collected (Shaw, 1999).

The data analysis utilized a set of techniques that included content analysis, pattern-matching, and explanation-building techniques (Yin, 2014). The content analysis involved listening to and transcribing the tapes, reading the transcripts to list the features associated with militancy by each owner-manager and establishing categories which were then developed into a systemic typology. These features included the root causes and the costs of conflicts.

Pattern-matching technique involved examining whether there were any interesting patterns and how the data related to what was expected (Yin, 2014). It also involved cross-case analysis and examining whether there were inconsistencies or contradictions between owner-managers' attitudes and what they do. Explanation-building technique allowed a series of linkages to be made and interpreted in light of the explanations provided by each respondent. This technique allowed the explanation of the findings to be built around the stories of business owners, enterprise agency executive and militant warlords. For example, body language and tone of voice on certain answers were put into consideration when analyzing the information gathered from the interviews.

Within this study, the coding process was inductive rather than being based on a set of preconceived, standardized codes. Categories and sub-categories were produced for indexing and the data derived from the case study firms. The codes took the form of 'code domains' which made explicit key contexts, actions, meanings, and relationships (Fisher, 2004), based on themes and processes identified from the transcribed interviews, whilst informed by the guiding frame of reference identified in the initial literature review, underpinning the study. The approach to coding allowed for ongoing modification of, and adjustment to, the framework which made up the codes as the research in the case studies unfolded. Moreover, this overall coding framework was a hierarchical ordering of the codes, which allows for the conducting of content analysis at different levels of aggregation (Fisher, 2004).

6. The effects of militancy

The conflict in the Delta is connected to oil exploitation in the region which results in environmental pollution and degradation. The impact of this crisis on enterprise development in the region was the subject of this study. The transcript of data collected from the interviews with the business owners, militant leaders (Commanders D, E, and F), and an Enterprise Agency executive operating in the Niger Delta region were inductively coded as discussed above. The emerging themes from this analysis are discussed below.

The profile of the case study companies and the summary findings from the interviews are presented in Table 1 with reference to Rettberg's costs of conflict from a business perspective (Rettberg, 2008, 2013) and discussed under the entrepreneurial theories outlined above.

[Insert Table 1 about here]

6.1 Extortion payments and threats

The case study firms were asked about the effects of militancy on their businesses. Threats and extortion payments were mentioned by Companies 1, 4, 5, 7, and 8 as the costs of the conflict. The responses suggest that the costs of the conflict varied according to company size, as the enterprise agency executive suggest:

> 'Although SMEs are generally targeted for extortion, enterprises are of different sizes and levels, you know! Say, if Shell is attacked, the conditions given to Shell will be different from those given to smaller enterprises unless they expect that the payment could come from a larger firm or government.' [Enterprise Agency Executive]

This may suggest that the larger the firm the greater the costs of conflict as confirmed by the owner-manager of Company 1, a marine transport business in the oil sector. Although larger companies were targeted for extortion payments, small businesses, such as market women and petty traders, were also victims. Apart from company size, the owner-managers of the case study firms indicated that the sector in which the businesses were located was the most important factor. The oil and gas-related SME sector tended to be mostly affected by the conflict. This was confirmed by the owner of the general contract company by saying:

> 'Well, not all small businesses in the region are affected on the same scale. But any small business that is involved in oil and gas servicing is being directly and badly affected in the region' [Company 8, General Contracts, Non-oil Sector]

The above quotes demonstrate the severe and direct impact of militancy on small businesses in the oil and gas sector. Although the quotes above indicate the oil and gas sector as the main target, there is evidence to suggest that location is significant in the violent conflict. With respect to location, business owners indicated that the 'core' Niger

Delta States (Nwogwugwu et al., 2012, p. 28) was mostly affected. The quotes above suggest that factors such as product, sector, and geographical location are among those that influence the extent of the costs of conflict.

6.2 Closure of businesses

Another direct cost of the crisis was the closure of businesses in the region, according to Companies 1, 2, 3, 6, and 8. The owner of these businesses variously indicated that that small businesses in the region have suffered the impact of the crisis through business closures which have rendered some people jobless and unemployed in the region. Likely, some of the business closures were not due to the crisis since many of the closures may be due to management issues rather than militancy.

6.3 Corruption

Although corruption is embedded in all fabric of the Nigerian society, the participants in the study commented particularly on the corruption directly attributed to the actions of oil companies (MNCs) in the Niger Delta region. They commented on how the oil companies were engaged in "payoffs and rewards" which are based on blackmail and connections:

"The MNCs are paying off and rewarding people they shouldn't. They are giving money people that do not matter in an attempt to pacify them. They shouldn't do this really" [Company 1, Marine Transport, Oil Sector].

The militant warlord (Commander D) also confirmed the role of the MNCs in the conflict by explaining how the MNCs ignored people that 'mattered' in the region and accorded recognition to some youths who had more disruptive power on oil production, causing mayhem, loss of lives, displacement of people, hijacking ships and helicopters, kidnaping MNCs staff, and vandalizing facilities to obtain pay-offs and ransoms from the oil companies. This reveals some of the common forms of violent attacks on enterprises (both large and small) in the region.

6.4 Loss of business opportunities and opportunity costs

The participants in the case study firms and key informants commented on the diminishing foreign direct investment which resulted in the loss of business opportunities in the region. They also commented on the security threat as the greatest challenge that hinders enterprise development in the Niger Delta. One of the participants commented as follows:

"Because of the militant activities in the region, foreign investors have left. They are no more business opportunities. There is security for them anymore and I don't blame them" [Company 4, Oil products Marketing, Oil Sector].

6.5 How SMEs were responding to the conflict in the Niger Delta

The owner-managers were asked about how they were dealing with the problems of militancy in the region. The findings as presented in table 1included public condemnation of violence and carrying on business as usual (Companies 2, 3, 5, and 6); supporting enterprise development (Companies 3, 4, 5, and 6); mentoring initiatives and microfinance (Companies 1, 4, 7, and 8); refusing to sell to militants (Companies 2, 3, 6, and 7); and philanthropy (Companies 2, 6, and 8). As we discussed above, Oetzel and Getz (2012) posit the possibility of both unilateral and collective responses. Findings here overwhelmingly suggest a collective response. For example, the owner-manager of Company 8 explained how, collectively, they have set about directly engaging militants:

'We have jointly put resources together to provide microcredit, enlightenment and most importantly mentoring initiatives aimed at transferring small business set-up and management skill sets to militants as a form of engagement. The microcredit helps in supporting grass-root enterprise activities such as agriculture with the potential to develop into a sustainable livelihood' [Company 8, General Contract, Non-Oil sector]

The above statement of pulling resources together to provide financial support and setting up a mentoring initiative aimed at transferring management skills to owner-managers is representative of the ways the study firms dealt with the conflict in the Niger Delta. This strategy is consistent with Oetzel and Getz (2012) supposition that firms may respond to violent conflict by supporting small business development through microfinance and skills training. They also argue that small firms of less than 100 employees are less likely to make a significant impact on an individual basis. "Pulling resources together" is consistent with Newsom's (2011) suggestion that actors in the Niger Delta should not operate in isolation but should combine levers and use each other's momentum to be effective. Column 9 of Table 1 represents the cross-case analysis of the responses.

Some of the respondents also indicated that they are supporting the government's 'Amnesty Programme' which is targeted at reintegrating the militants into mainstream society and economy. Specifically, the owner-managers of Companies 3, 6, and 7 were supporting the program because it will give the militants an equal opportunity to belong to and be employed by the government. The owner of a catering service also said that they refuse to sell to or serve those who facilitate the conflict. Although the participant firms were eager to point out how they were dealing with the challenges posed by militancy in the region, it could also be argued that seeking conflict resolutions might be disadvantageous to the firms by attracting competitors to the area (Renouard & Lado, 2012).

7. Discussion

The study aimed to explore the effect of militancy on local SMEs and how the businesses were dealing with the crisis. Based on the fieldwork evidence presented in this study, the perspectives offered by the resource-based and social behavioral theories and Rettberg's costs of conflict framework, discussed above, appear useful in understanding entrepreneurial behavior and responsiveness to social and environmental issues. William, Combs, and Ketchen (2014) argues that the resource-based theory has merit as a complementary explanation for entrepreneurship. In this section, we explore how these theoretical perspectives fit with the empirical results.

The study identifies the direct costs of the conflict (which include extortion payments, threats, direct attacks on the companies, and business closures) and the indirect costs (including loss of business opportunities and lack of infrastructure). These costs are consistent with those identified by Rettberg (2008). However, the study also identifies other costs of the conflict which complement Rettberg's, such as loss of human lives, displacement of people (particularly women and children), and material destruction.

Company-specific characteristics such as company size, sector and location suggest differences in how entrepreneurial activity is affected by the costs of the conflict in the Niger Delta. Those who reported severe impact included larger enterprises. These categories of SMEs were more prone to becoming victims of extortion and other forms of attack. These actions led to closure of business units and losses as well as folding-up of enterprises. This was consistent with Rettberg's (2008) finding that larger companies were more likely to report costs associated with armed conflict than were smaller ones.

However, it is difficult to know the extent to which the closures were purely a result of the conflict rather than such factors as poor management skills, which include networking skills to facilitate access to resources and understanding which the owner-manager lacks.

In contrast, smaller or micro businesses were not subjected to the same level of costs, in proportion to their size, as their larger counterparts. This does not mean that small size functioned as a buffer of militants' attacks (Rettberg et al., 2010). For example, Abdelnour et al. (2008), Eze (2011) and Rettberg's (2013) assert that market women, petty traders, fast food sellers, and other small and grass-root businesses have witnessed a downturn in their operations as a result of violent conflicts.

The costs of the conflict in the study also depended on the sector in which the business operated. Enterprises in the oil and gas-related small business sector tended to be severely affected by the violent agitations of the Niger Delta militants, while other sectors and generic groups have also suffered some mild or indirect costs. This finding is also consistent with the Columbian conflict study in which companies in the mining, gas, electricity, agriculture, and transportation sectors most frequently reported the direct costs related to armed conflict, while financial services and investors reported the least (Rettberg, 2008). However, it can be argued that costs have not been evenly spread. For example, the degree to which the sector is labor-intensive and/or oriented toward international markets can determine how the conflict has affected companies (Rettberg, 2013).

The case study firms indicated that the location of the businesses was also an important determinant of the costs of the conflict in relation to the 'core' Niger Delta region that is, Bayelsa, Delta, and Rivers states (Nwogwugwu et al., 2012, p. 28). Therefore, businesses that are located outside these core areas were not directly affected by the costs of the conflict. In previous studies, the highest direct costs to the private sector were reported in cities in the country's conflict-affected area, while the capital appeared to be a relatively peaceful oasis for economic activity (Dai et al., 2013; Getz & Oetzel, 2010; Rettberg, 2008).

There was support for our assumption from the resource-based theory that surmised that enterprises in the Niger Delta and in other developing areas are constrained by both a restricted extrinsic resource base such as limited access to raw material and capital and intrinsic resource base such as a limited pool of skills and experience, which is exacerbated by militant action.

In this study, the lack of resources, such as finance posed a significant challenge for small businesses in the region. The loss of compensation from the Nigerian state for the loss of land and from the MNCs for the environmental pollution and degradation constituted a constrained resource base. Compensation money as well as increased revenue allocation can definitely provide a good source of developmental and start-up capital for small businesses in the region, given that access to finance is a major problem for SMEs, especially in developing countries (North, Baldock, & Ekanem, 2010). As we saw from our finding, militant action further compromised available resources influencing both availability of resources and their costs.

There is also support for our assumption from social behavior theory that the environment and infrastructure, such as social networks are important in SME developing, often relying on local communities and kinship connections in developing regions. Such networks will help to counter the negative effects of militant conflict on local enterprise development.

The poor quality infrastructure and erratic supply of electricity in the developing countries have a major impact on SME development (Nwosu et al., 2013). A number of research studies conducted in Nigeria (for example, Aina, 2007; Nwosu et al., 2013) has identified that less than 20% of the Nigerian population have access to the stable electricity supply. According to some estimates, the region has generated about 500 USD billion in the past 50 years for the Nigerian economy (Obi, 2010). This provides a sharp contrast between the amount of wealth generated from the region and its poor state of infrastructure.

Enterprise development and sustainability in developing countries can be influenced by the stance the government takes with respect to encouraging people to start and develop their own businesses and through the behavior of politicians and government officials in their dealing with entrepreneurs and would-be entrepreneurs. This is undoubtedly fundamental and important for developing countries because the way entrepreneurs and would-be entrepreneurs are viewed and treated can be either enabling or constraining (BIS, 2013; Eze, 2011).

The dynamics and challenges of resource conflicts have compelled the MNCs to provide benefits as a means of dousing the agitation, pacifying the region, and creating a safer and more peaceful environment for business (Ikelegbe, 2005). However, as demonstrated in the case study interviews, the approach hardly achieves the intended purpose. The challenges of creating and ensuring access to these benefits have fueled a deadly struggle among various groups of people in the community as each group struggles to prove their relevance and capacity to disrupt the oil economy (Ikelegbe, 2005). This action undoubtedly leads to greed and corruption and does not help in providing a stable and conducive environment (Zyglidopoulos, 2016), advocated in social behavioral theory, for sustainable enterprises in the Niger Delta region. Collier and Hoeffler (2002) argue that conflicts may be explained either by grievance or greed and conclude that if we want to understand the causes of contemporary civil wars we should ignore explanations based on grievances and look instead at the greed of the rebel groups. Therefore, greed rather than grievance may be partly responsible for the conflict in the Niger Delta.

The crisis in the Niger Delta region arising from the activities of the different militant groups operating in the region has brought about some negative implications for enterprises in the region with respect to foreign direct investments. The kidnapping of foreigners and other forms of attack do not provide a safe business environment, but have the effect of scaring away potential foreign investors and has robbed the region and indeed the Nigerian state of the benefits of such investments and opportunities which small businesses and entrepreneurs could take advantage of (Nwogwugwu et al. 2012). These actions result in the loss of business opportunities and opportunity costs as identified by Rettberg (2008). Therefore, there are complementarity relationships between foreign investments and business start-up and development in struggling and developing economies (Thompson & Zang, 2015).

The study firms indicated how they were actually dealing with the crisis arising from militancy and their willingness to take control of their destiny by engaging in conflict reduction. Some of the responses were, however, not strategic, such as providing room for youth engagement and mentoring initiative. This finding was not surprising considering the size of the firm. It supports Oetzel and Getz (2012) theory which states that firms with 100 employees or fewer were significantly less likely to strategically respond to violent conflict since such firms may lack the capacity or resources to respond strategically. However, it must be pointed out that the conflict-mitigating initiatives focused on reducing the negative effects of conflict, rather than actually resolving it (Getz & Oetzel, 2010). Therefore, the level of resources devoted to the initiatives by the firms was minimal. It can also be argued that youth engagement may not necessarily lead to more entrepreneurship.

Other forms of the response to the conflict included the provision of financial help, philanthropy, public condemnation of violence, and continuing business activities as usual. These forms of responses appear to be more strategic and capable of helping to obtain long-term competitive advantage and/or positive financial outcomes (Branzei & Abdelnour, 2010).

Finally, it is worth pointing out that the businesses in the study were collaborating together and with other stakeholders to solve the challenges because they were not able to have a major impact on their own. The interventions were also not proactively identified and pursued as they were merely peripheral to their core business and they were haphazardly reacting to situations. The initiatives were more effective when they involved the government, NGOs, and other SMEs. This is consistent with Oetzel et al.'s (2010) argument that partnerships between the private sector and NGOs can provide complementary skills, competencies, and capacities to engage in social change. Bottenberg, Tuschke, and Flickinger (2017) also argue that an institutionally anchored stakeholder management can have a number of advantages.

8. Conclusion

The results of the study provide a better understanding of the impact of the Niger Delta armed conflict on SMEs in the region, the extent to which the costs of conflict identified by Rettberg (2008, 2013) are present in the study, how SMEs respond to the militancy, and the implications for developing countries. It also contributes to theories of entrepreneurship which are applied in the study to explain findings.

One valuable contribution of this study is that it looks at a business activity to which few academic researchers, practitioners, or policymakers have direct access. The study also contributes to the work of the few researchers who have looked at the costs of conflict (Rettberg, 2008, 2013) and strategic response to violent conflict (Branzei & Abdelnour, 2010; Kolt & Lenfant, 2010; Oetzel & Getz, 2012).

Developing countries such as Sudan, Algeria, and Angola are lagging behind in dealing with the threat posed by MNCs to the environment because of poor governance, economic diversification, and lack of quality institutions as identified in the Niger Delta conflict (Frynas, Wood, & Hinks, 2017; Newsom, 2011). Therefore, to reduce violent conflict, these developing countries should take more cooperative approaches by pulling resources together and developing the required capacities for environmental impact assessment, disaster prevention and management, and emergency preparedness.

Therefore, it is argued that businesses in developing economies should become a more involved with social issues by finding solutions to problems (Eweje, 2006). The findings in this study demonstrate that businesses in developing countries can respond positively to crisis and contribute to SME development. Thus, this paper contributes to research on the literature on business under crisis.

A firm that voluntarily responds to violent conflict as a first-mover, may achieve a position that strengthens its legitimacy and ultimately leads to a long-term competitive advantage (Oetzel & Getz, 2012). When the situation in the country improves, the firm may have advantages stemming from good relations with the community, leading to greater access to preferential opportunities for expansion.

This study has some limitations that suggest a direction for future research. First and foremost, the study was based on snowballing samples, and thus it is not clear whether the views of the participants represent those of the larger populations. In the second instance, due to the difficulty of identifying the militants, we were only able to interview three militants. Finally, there were only eight firms in the study, making it a small sample size. However, since the study is an explorative work, it has value as a large-scale study that would help to demonstrate the wider application of the research results.

Disclosure statement

No potential conflict of interest was reported by the authors.

References

Abdelnour, S., Badri, B., El Jack, A., Wheeler, D., McGrath, S., & Branzei, O. (2008). *Examining enterprise capacity: A participatory social assessment in Darfur and Southern Sudan*. Toronto: Centre for Refugee Studies. York University.

Abdelnour, S., & Branzei, O. (2009). The renaissance of community enterprise in postwar Sudan. *ASAC*, *30*(21), 1–24.

Aina, O. C. (2007). The role of SMEs in poverty alleviation in Nigeria. *Journal of Land Use and Development Studies*, *3*(1), 124–131.

Anyadike-Daness, M., Hart, M., & Du, J. (2013). Firm dynamics and job creation in the UK, *ERC White Paper No.6*.

Barney, J. (1991). Firm resources and sustained competitive advantage. *Journal of Management*, *17*(1), 99–120.

Baskerville, R. F. (2003). Hofstede never studied culture. *Accounting, Organizations and Society, 28* (1), 1–14.

Berkes., F., & Adhikari., T. (2006). Development and conservation: Indigenous businesses and the UNDP equator initiative. *Int. J. Entrepreneurship and Small Business, 3*(6), 671–690.

BIS. (2013). SME: The key enablers of business success and the economic rationale for government intervention. *Department of Business Innovation and Skills Analysis Paper, No.2.*

Bottenberg, K., Tuschke, A., & Flickinger, M. (2017). Corporate governance between shareholder and stakeholder orientation: Lesson from Germany. *Journal of Management Inquiry, 26*(2), 165–180.

Branzei, O., & Abdelnour, S. (2010). Another day, another dollar: Enterprise resilience under terrorism in developing countries. *Journal of International Business Studies, 41*(5), 804–825.

Collier, P. (2007). Economic causes of civil conflict and their implications for policy. In C. A. Crocker, F. O. Hampson, & P. Aall (Eds.), *Learning the dogs of war: Conflict management in a divided world* (pp. 197–218). Washington DC: United Institute of Peace.

Collier, P., & Hoeffler, A. (2002). Greed and grievance in African civil wars. *CSAE Working Paper No. WPS/2002-01.* Oxford: Centre for African Economies.

Corbin, J. M., & Strauss, A. L. (2008). *Basics of qualitative research: Techniques and procedures for developing grounded theory.* Thousand Oaks, California: Sage.

Crawford, G. C., Dimov, D., & McKelvey, B. (2016). Realism, empiricism, and fetishism in the study of entrepreneurship. *Journal of Management Inquiry, 25*(2), 168–170.

Dai, L., Eden, L., & Beamish, P. (2013). Place, space and geographical exposure: Foreign subsidiary survival in conflict zones. *Journal of International Business Studies, 44*(6), 554–578.

Dana, L.-P. (2015). Indigenous entrepreneurship: An emerging field of research. *International Journal of Business and Globalisation, 14*(2), 158–169.

Ekanem, I. (2007). Insider accounts: A qualitative research method for small firms. *Journal of Small Business and Enterprise Development, 14*(1), 105–117.

Eweje, G. (2006). Environmental costs and responsibilities resulting from oil exploitation in developing countries: The case of the Niger Delta of Nigeria. *Journal of Business Ethics, 69,* 27–56.

Eze, M. C. (2011). The political economy of conflict resolution in a natural resource economy: The case of Nigeria's Niger Delta. *African Journal of Political Science and International Relations, 5* (3), 152–158.

Fischer, E., & Reuber, A. R. (2011). Social interaction via new social media: (How) can interactions on Twitter affect effectual thinking and behaviour? *Journal of Business Venturing, 26,* 1–18.

Fisher, C. (2004). *Researching and Writing a Dissertation.* New Jersey: FT Prentice Hall.

Frynas, J. G., Wood, G., & Hinks, T. (2017). The resource curse without natural resources: Expectations of resource booms and their impact. *African Affairs,* 1–28. doi:10.1093/afraf/adx001

Getz, K. A., & Oetzel, J. (2010). MNE strategic intervention in violent conflict: Variations based on conflict characteristics. *Journal of Business Ethics, 89*(4), 375–386.

Grant, R. M. (2003). Strategic planning in a turbulent environment: Evidence from the oil majors. *Strategic Management Journal, 24*(6), 491–517.

Ihua, U. B. (2009). SMEs key failure-factors: A comparison between the United Kingdom and Nigeria. *Journal of Social Science, 18*(3), 199–207.

Ihua, U. B. (2010). Local content policy and SMEs sector promotion: The Nigerian oil industry experience. *International Journal of Business and Management, 5*(5), 3–13.

Ikelegbe, A. (2005). The economy of the conflict in the oil rich Niger Delta region of Nigeria. *Nordic Journal of African Studies, 14*(2), 208–234.

Jamali, D., & Mirshak, R. (2010). Business-conflict linkages: Revisiting MNCs, CSR, and conflict. *Journal of Business Ethics, 93*(3), 443–464.

Kolt, A., & Lenfant, F. (2010). MNC reporting on CSR and conflict in Central Africa. *Journal of Business Ethics, 93*(2), 241–255.

Luo, Y. (2006). Political behaviour, social responsibility, and perceived corruption: A structuration perspective. *Journal of International Business Studies, 37*(6), 747–766.

Newbert, S. L. (2007). Empirical research on the resource-based view of the firm: An assessment and suggestions for future research. *Strategic Management Journal, 28*(2), 121–146.

Newsom, C. 2011. *Conflict in the Niger Delta: More than a local affair*. United States Institute of peace, USA. Special report. 271. 1–18.

North, D., Baldock, R., & Ekanem, I. (2010). Is there a debt finance gap relating to Scottish SMEs? A demand-side Perspective. *Venture Capital, 12*(3), 173–192.

Nwogwugwu, N., Alao, O. E., & Egwuonwu, C. (2012). Militancy and Insecurity in the Niger Delta: Impact on the inflow of foreign direct investment to Nigeria. *Kuwait Chapter of Arabian Journal of Business and Management Review, 2*(1), 23–37.

Nwosu, A. C., Ukoha, O. O., Iheke, O.R., Emenyonu, C.A., Lemchi, J.I., Ohajianya, D.O., & Emenyonu, C.C. (2013). Funding youth entrepreneurship in SMEs: A panacea for youth unemployment in Niger-Delta, Nigeria, *ICBE-RF Research Report N0. 63/13*.

Obi, C. (2010). Oil extraction, dispossession, resistance, and conflict in Nigeria's oil-rich Niger Delta. *Canadian Journal of Development Studies, 30*(1–2), 219–236.

Oetzel, J., & Getz, K. (2012). Why and how might firms respond strategically to violent conflict? *Journal of International Business Studies, 43*, 166–186.

Oetzel, J., Westermann-Behalo, M., Koerber, C., Fort, T. L., & Rivera, J. (2010). Business and Peace: Sketching the terrain. *Journal of Business Ethics, 89*, 351–373.

Peredo, A. M., & McLean, M. (2010). Indigenous development and the cultural captivity of entrepreneurship. *Business & Society, 52*(4), 1–37.

Renouard, C., & Lado, H. (2012). CSR and inequality in the Niger Delta (Nigeria), corporate governance. *The International Journal of Business in Society, 12*(4), 472–484.

Rettberg, A. (2008). Exploring the peace dividend: Perceptions of armed conflict impacts on the Colombian private sector: Results from a national survey, Spanish Report, International Alert & Universidad de los Andes, March 2008.

Rettberg, A. (2013). Peace is better business, and business makes better peace: The role of the private sector in Colombian peace processes. *GIGA Working Paper*, No. 240.

Rettberg, A., Leiteritz, R., & Nasi, C. (2010). Entrepreneurial activity and civil war in Colombia: Exploring the mutual determinants between armed conflict and the private sector, United Nations university. *Working Paper* No. 2010/06.

Reynolds, P. D. (1991). Sociology and entrepreneurship: Concepts and contributions". *Entrepreneurship: Theory & Practice, 16*(2), 47–70.

Robson, C. (2002). *Real World research: A resource for social-scientists and practitioner-researchers*. Oxford: Blackwell.

Shane, S. A. (1994). The effect of national culture on the choice between licensing and direct foreign investment. *Strategic Management Journal, 15*, 627–642.

Shaw, E. (1999). A guide to the qualitative research process: Evidence from a small firm study. *Qualitative Market Research: An International Journal, 2*(2), 59–70.

Spence, L. J., & Rutherford, R. (2001). Social responsibility, profit maximisation and the small firm owner-manager. *Journal of Small Business and Enterprise Development, 8*(2), 126–139.

Thompson, P., & Zang, W. (2015). Foreign direct investment and the SME sector. *International Journal of Entrepreneurial Behavior and Research, 21*(1), 50–75.

William, E. G., Combs, J. G., & Ketchen, J. D. J. (2014). Using resource-based theory to help explain plural form franchising. *Entrepreneurship Theory and Practice, 38*(3), 449–472.

Yin, R. (2014). *Case study research: Design and methods*. London: Sage.

Zyglidopoulos, S. (2016). Towards a theory of second-order corruption. *Journal of Management Inquiry, 25*(1), 3–10.

Index

Page numbers followed by "n" denote endnotes.

Abdelnour, S. 94, 95
Ademilua, A. V. 36
Adenugba, A. A. 36
Adersua, A. 56
Adhikari, T. 94
Africa 2–5, 28, 57, 75, 78, 84
African business 1–3
African Business Development 4, 5
African Development Bank 74, 78
African economies 74, 75, 77–79, 83, 84
African Informal Entrepreneurial Revolution 74
Ahmad, N. H. 36, 42, 44
Akira, K. 33
Alessandra, T. 33
Allan, I. S. 2
alleviate poverty 3, 9, 11, 12, 14, 15, 18, 19, 21–23
Amankwah-Amoah, J. 52
Amirah, N. A. 29
Anderson, R. B. 22
armed conflict 94, 104, 106
Arregle, J.-L. 54, 59
Aruni, W. 33

Bartlett, C. A. 32
Bartlett, J. E. 35
basket weaving business 11, 16, 18, 20
basket weaving enterprise 9, 11–24
Baum, J. R. 32, 33, 43
Becker, G. S. 56n2
Berkes., F. 94
Bird, B. 31, 32
Bohné, T. M. 29
Bottenberg, K. 106
Branzei, O. 95
Brush, C. G. 56
business closures 102, 104
business environment 28–30, 34, 35, 37, 42, 44, 45, 82, 85
business opportunities 80, 94, 102, 104, 106
business owners 95, 96, 100, 101
business performance 32, 33, 43

Chandler, G. 32–33
children 13, 15–19, 22, 23, 55, 58, 104
Chrisman, J.J. 12
closures 102, 104
Cohen, J. 41
Coleman, S. 56
Collier, P. 105
Combs, J. G. 103
communities 10–13, 15–24, 94
community-based enterprises 11, 12, 19, 22–24
community-based informal enterprises 15, 19
companies 93, 94, 101–104
competencies 4, 29, 31, 32, 41, 43, 44, 81, 82, 106
conflict 92–95, 100–107
control variables 58
corruption 34, 57, 68, 84, 92, 102, 105
costs 21, 52, 67, 93, 94, 100, 101, 104, 105; of conflict 94, 100–102, 106, 107
Covin, J.G. 43

Dana, L.-P. 12, 22, 94
data analysis method 59
Dauda, R. S. 10
Davies, R. 1
dependent variable 58, 59, 62, 64
Dolz, C. 44

Eckhardt, J. T. 9
ecological resilience 4, 75, 76
economic issues 3, 9, 15
ecosystem resilience 75, 77, 82–85
educated entrepreneurs 53, 54, 67
Elegbede, T. 53
entrepreneurial activities 4, 9, 10, 35, 51, 56, 57, 68, 75, 85, 93
entrepreneurial competence/competencies 3, 29–35, 37, 39, 41–46
entrepreneurial education 3, 4
entrepreneurial human capital 3, 4, 51, 52
entrepreneurial intentions 75, 81
entrepreneurial orientation 33, 41, 82

INDEX

entrepreneurial resource mobilization 67, 69
entrepreneurial resources 56, 81
entrepreneurial theory 93
entrepreneurship ecosystem 74, 76
entrepreneurship education 4, 81, 84, 85
entrepreneurship research 2
environmental dynamism 35, 41, 42, 44
ethnic entrepreneurship 23
extortion payments 94, 101, 104

Fabrizio, G. 33
Fajana, S. 53
family situation 55, 56, 58
Feldman, M. 80
female entrepreneurs 55, 56, 63, 66–68
firm's response 95
Flickinger, M. 106
formal education 52–58, 62–64, 66, 67
Fornell, C. G. 37
founders education 53
frugal innovations 4, 75, 79, 85

Gaganis, C. 36
Gbajumo-Sheriff, M. 53
gender differences 52, 55–57, 63, 64, 68
gender discrimination 11, 15, 18–21, 23
Getz, K. A. 95, 103, 106
Ghoshal, S. 32
Gimeno, J. 66
global entrepreneurship 35
Gümüsay, A. A. 29
Gwadabe, U. M. 29

Higgins, C. C. 35
Hinson, R. E. 33
Hironori, Y. 33
Hoeffler, A. 105
Honig, B. 22
Hood, J. N. 33
Horak, S. 53
Huang, Y. 53
hypothesis testing 60

Ibidunni, A. S. 34, 36
Ibidunni, O. S. 34, 36
Iborra, M. 44
Ibrahim, M. 33
Ifere, S. E. 52
Igbo rural community women 10
Igbos 8–15, 18, 20, 21
Igbo women 9–13, 19, 22
Igbo women basketry entrepreneurs 15, 19
Igbo women basket weaving entrepreneurs 13, 15, 17–19, 21
Igbo women entrepreneurs 3, 15, 18, 19
Igbo women's basket weaving enterprise 9, 11
Igwe, P. A. 12, 23, 54, 79

independent variables 58–60, 63
indigenous entrepreneurship 23, 94
informal entrepreneurial learning 3, 15, 16, 19, 20, 22, 23
informal entrepreneurs 33–35, 39, 41, 81, 82, 84
informal entrepreneurship 15, 75, 79, 81
informality 2, 3, 29, 77, 78, 81, 83, 84
informal sector, in Africa 2, 4, 5
informal SMEs 3, 4, 28–31, 33, 42–44
informal ties 4, 52–56, 58, 62–64, 68, 69
innovation performance 29, 36, 37, 41–44, 46; of informal entrepreneurs 34, 35, 41; of SMEs 30, 33–35, 45
institutional logic 75, 79, 80
Isenberg, D. J. 74, 82
Iyiola, O. 36

Jansen, E. 32, 33
Jansen, J. J. P. 36
Justo, R. 56

Kabongo, J. 2
Kedir, A. M. 2
Kesinro, O. R. 36
Ketchen, J. D. J. 103
Khayesi, J. N. 52
Kotrlik, I. J. W. 35
Kuada, J. 1
Kummerow, L. 36

Larcker, D. F. 37
Lewin, K. 67
Lindsay, P. 32
Locke, E. A. 32
Lowe, N. 80
Luo, Y. 53

Madichie, N. O. 2, 33, 54, 56
Man, T. W. Y. 32, 33, 36
Matthews, C. H. 23
militancy 4, 92, 95, 96, 100–103, 106; effects of 92, 101, 103
militants 93, 96, 100, 103, 104, 107
Mitchell, R. K. 32
Mitchelmore, S. 32, 43
moderating variables 58, 63
Moser, S. B. 23
Mosey, S. 42

Nafziger, E. W. 54
Newsom, C. 103
Niger Delta 92–96, 100–107
Nigeria 2, 3, 8–10, 12, 13, 17, 29, 30, 44, 52, 54, 57, 68
Nilsson, K. 2
Nyuur, R. B. 52

INDEX

Obaji, N. O. 35
Obiwuru, T. C. 34
Oetzel, J. 95, 103, 106
Ogundele, J. K. 34
Okwu, A. T. 34
Olugu, M. U. 35
Oluwalaiye, O. B. 34
Ortiz-Ospina, E. 10
Otoo, M. 2
Owoyemi, O. 53

Paolo, G. 33
Pasiouras, F. 36
pattern-matching technique 100
Peredo, A. M. 12, 22
policy implications 23, 75
poverty 10–12, 14, 17–20, 22, 23, 84, 85; alleviation 3, 4, 8–10, 12, 22, 23
productive entrepreneurial ecosystem 80
public policy 68

Ramayah, T. 36
Rasmussen, E. 42, 43
Ratten, V. 12, 22
relationship competencies 37, 44
resource-based theory 93, 103, 104
resource mobilization 3, 4, 51, 66–68
Rettberg, A. 93, 94, 104, 106
Reynolds, P. D. 93
Rezat, S. 15
Robb, A. 56
Robson, C. 96
robustness tests 63
Roser, M. 10
Rowley, J. 32, 43
rural Igbo communities 10–12, 22–24
rural Igbo women 19, 22, 23; entrepreneurs 22, 24
Rutashobya, L. K. 2

Safón, V. 44
Sen, A. K. 10, 17
Shane, S. A. 9
Shepherd, D. A. 10, 32
Slevin, D.P. 43
small and medium enterprises (SMEs) 28–30, 33–36, 44, 45, 92–95, 105, 106
Smith, K. G. 32
socio-cultural issues 3, 8, 15
Spring, A. 1
Stuart, R. 32

Tendai, C. 29
Thurlow, J. 1
traditional barriers 15, 18–21, 23
Tuschke, A. 106

unproductive entrepreneurial ecosystems 4, 80

Van Den Bosch, F. A. 36
variables 41, 58, 62–64, 77
Volberda, H. W. 36
Vollstedt, M. 15
Voulgari, F. 36

Wang, S. L. 53
Welter, F. 33
William, E. G. 103
Williams, C. C. 2
Wilson, C. 36
Woldie, A. 56
women entrepreneurs 10–18, 21, 56, 66
women entrepreneurship 4, 8, 9, 11, 15, 17, 23, 24
Wright, M. 42

Young, J. E. 33

Zizile, T. 29

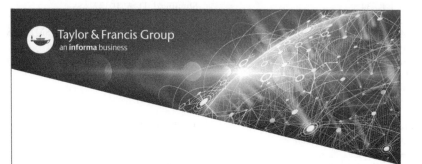